Montana's BIG SKY COUNTRY

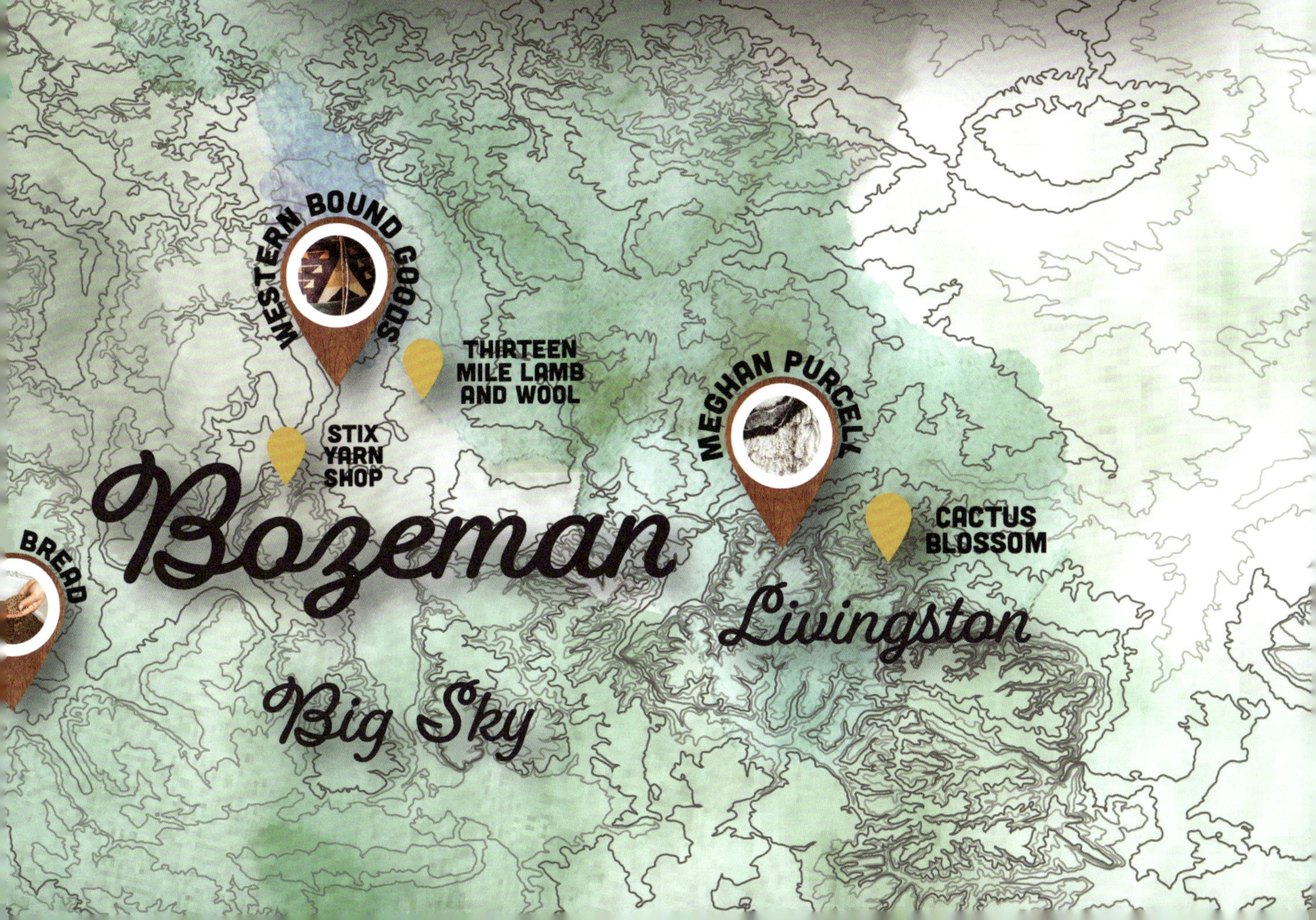

WESTERN BOUND GOODS

THIRTEEN MILE LAMB AND WOOL

STIX YARN SHOP

MEGHAN PURCELL

CACTUS BLOSSOM

BREAD

Bozeman

Livingston

Big Sky

Author and Creative Director: Andrea Hungerford
Photographer: Lauren Lipscomb
Production Editor: Hannah Thiessen
Patterns and Projects Designers: Shellie Anderson, Leah Angle, Andrea Hungerford, Irina Pi, Kjerste Whaley, Renate Yerkes
Recipe: Stella Moss
Pattern Technical Editors: Meaghan Corwin and Alexandra Viegel
Models: Daniel Sanabria, Anna Vanuga, Alexandra Weeden
Stylist: Kristi Reed / Windy Peak Vintage
Montana Map: Topography design by PEAKS (*peaksonpoint.com*), watercolor overlay and graphics by Hannah Thiessen
Printer: B&B Print Source

COPYRIGHT

Text and photographs copyright 2019 by Blueberry Hill. All rights reserved. No part of this publication may be reproduced, distributed or transmitted in any form or by any means, including photocopying or other electronic methods without written permission from the author.

ORDERING INFORMATION

By Hand is published three times annually. Subscriptions or single-issue purchases can be ordered online at: www.byhandserial.com.

Wholesale inquiries may be submitted via e-mail to www.nnkpress.com (North American distribution) or julie.asselin@yahoo.ca (Canadian distribution).

Published by Blueberry Hill
www.byhandserial.com
info@byhandserial.com

You can also find us on:
Ravelry at www.ravelry.com/groups/by-hand-serial
Facebook at www.facebook.com/byhandserial
Instagram at www.instagram.com/byhandserial

PRINTED IN THE USA

This book is printed on sustainably sourced paper at a wind-power optioned facility that practices 100% recycling of all waste materials. The paper in this publication contains fibers from well managed and responsibly harvested forests that meet strict environmental and socioeconomic standards.

Cover photo: Looking out over Blodgett Canyon and the Sapphire Mountains from the top of the Blodgett Overlook trail. Opposite page: The Bitterroot River flows through the Bitterroot Valley.

By Hand
making communities

Lookbook No. 10: Montana's Big Sky Country

Table Of Contents

Montana's Big Sky Country   2

Making Communities   4

On the Farm:
Montana Wool Works   7

Wooden Watercraft:
Morley Canoes   11

Knitting Pattern: Big Sky Ruana   14

Reclaimed Art Inspired by Nature:
Ruby & Revolver   19

Knitting Pattern: Castilleja Wrap   22

Knitting Pattern:
Pebble Shore Beanie   26

Felted Wool Artistry:
Meghan Purcell   33

Sewing Projects: Pendleton Buckets   36

Bags for Adventure:
Western Bound Goods   39

Knitting Pattern: Candice Cardigan   44

Hand Dyed:
The Farmers Daughter Fibers   47

Knitting Pattern:
Gallatin Wraparound   50

Local Yarn Stores of Montana   58

Artisan Textiles: Aporta Shop   59

Botanical Dyeing   62

Knitting Pattern:
Lewisia Handwarmers   66

From Scratch:
Stella German Organic Bakery   73

In the Kitchen: Autumn Panzanella   76

Montana Destinations   78

Macramé: Nona & Co   83

Macramé Project:
Hanging Planter   86

Montana Star Quilts   90

Glossary   92

Author/Creative Director Andrea Hungerford

Andrea Hungerford loves knitting for both the solitude it provides and the community it builds. Most all of her remaining time is spent with her three teenage daughters, who have taught her to navigate and even occasionally embrace the crazy chaos of everyday life. Her summertime homes away from home are the San Juan Islands and the coast of Maine, and her favorite place to scuba dive is Turks & Caicos, where she once swam with a whale shark. She hates to cook but loves to bake, and learns to navigate any new city she visits by locating the best bakery in town and going from there. She has cultivated a large and unwieldy garden at her home in the countryside, and loves to pick lilacs and peonies in the spring, sweet cherry tomatoes in the summer, and pink, red, and orange dahlias in the fall. She cares passionately about the environment and believes that there is no greater cause than protecting the natural world for future generations.

Photographer Lauren Lipscomb

Lauren Lipscomb is a Montana-based freelance photographer, specializing in a combination of elegant, editorial portraiture and environmental photojournalism. Born in California and raised in Alaska, Lauren's approach to photography has been shaped by both the landscapes and the people of the American West. She is deeply connected to her clients, subjects, and the earth, and inspired by the wilderness of her Montana home.

Production Editor Hannah Thiessen

Southern-born and bred, Hannah Thiessen is a self-proclaimed yarn obsessive, dabbling in knitting, crochet, weaving, spinning and sewing. She works day-to-day in the yarn industry, helping brands realize their creative potential, and is the author of *Slow Knitting*, a book focused on the beauty of making by hand. In her role as *By Hand Serial's* Production Editor, Hannah coordinates our designs and drives the visuals for our styled shoots and social media.

Montana's Big Sky Country

During the weeks spent traveling in Montana, I stumbled across many wonderful places. Our journey began in Bozeman, where we stayed at The Lark: a hip reinterpretation of a 1950s motor lodge. Ideally located on Bozeman's Main Street, lined with restaurants and locally-stocked shops, The Lark has wonderfully large common areas and two essentials that are actually located on-property: Treeline Coffee Roasters, a spacious and welcoming coffee shop stocked with locally roasted beans, and The Genuine Ice Cream Co., a refurbished airstream trailer serving up Bozeman's best locally made ice cream. Just a short walk from The Lark is Emerson Center for the Arts & Culture, an historic red brick school building that now houses artists' studios, galleries, and all manner of art classes for both children and adults.

Traveling a short distance from Bozeman through the aptly-named Paradise Valley, we reached the town of Livingston in only half an hour. In many ways, Livingston embodies small-town Montana life at its best: close proximity to Yellowstone National Park, a quaint and walkable downtown with art galleries and well-stocked bookstores, historical sites around every corner, and some of Montana's most stunning rivers and mountain ranges just outside its boundaries. While there, we discovered Cactus Blossom Collective, the brick and mortar branch of Windy Peak Vintage. The store was chock-full of vintage and independently designed clothing, small batch self-care products, and handcrafted artisan goods. Owner Kristi Reed thoughtfully curates each item, and the shop includes a selection of work from Montana artisans, as well.

In Whitefish, we were lucky enough to be in town for the opening of Fleur Bake Shop, a delicious bakery housed in a lovely space. The sight of the miles and miles of orchards along the banks of Flathead Lake raised my hopes for fresh cherries, but I was disappointed to learn that we were too early to enjoy the Flathead cherry harvest. While the scenery we experienced in Glacier National Park was stunning – albeit marred by poor weather – the crowds were overwhelming, even in late June when the Going-to-the-Sun Road had only just opened. Although Yellowstone and Glacier are the two national parks in Montana, they comprise only a small fraction of of the state's public lands. Western Montana's public lands offer hundreds of miles of trails, lush forests, serene and remote wilderness. The Bob Marshall Wilderness Area, for example, is comprised of more than one million acres of roadless land, rich wildlife habitat, and endless hiking and camping opportunities. I would be inclined to skip the crowded, better-known locales and opt for a more authentic Montana experience in one of these less-famous tracts of public land.

Similarly, while Flathead Lake was a glorious sight – it is the largest natural freshwater lake west of the Mississippi, after all – I was more taken with Swan Lake, tucked away off of the major north-to-south highway, anchored at the north by the town of Bigfork and offering miles of watery nooks and crannies to explore without the crowds that Flathead Lake attracts.

Finally, we ended our travels in the Bitterroot Valley, with an awe-inspiring hike to Blodgett Canyon Overlook, from which we could see the snow-capped Sapphire Mountains and the entire Bitterroot Valley spread out below us, followed by a much-deserved trip to Missoula's Sweet Peaks Ice Cream. We missed Aporta Shop's mid-summer grand opening, but soon visitors will be able to shop its beautiful collection of fiber and fabric goods made by artisans (many of whom are local makers) and by owner Noelle Sharp herself. In addition, Aporta Shop will stock a thoughtful variety of apothecary products, home goods, and, jewelry, and the weaving, knitting, and making classes offered there will make it a not-to-be-missed Missoula destination. As the shop's website proclaims, "Aporta fibers are handpicked to ensure all products are of the highest caliber. Aporta honors the tradition of honest, hard work."

Our trip was not all smooth sailing – there is no doubt that Montana weather is unreliable, even in the summer. Our hopes of hiking in Big Sky and spending time on the Gallatin River were dashed by five inches of snow – on the summer solstice, no less! And our travels throughout the state were frequently interrupted by thunderstorms and bouts of heavy rainfall. But the storm clouds were spectacularly dramatic over the mountain ranges, and most days, the sun found a way to peek through the clouds by day's end.

Opposite page: One of the Flathead Valley's many lakes.
Following page: Fields of canola bloom bright yellow under darkening stormclouds.

Making Communities

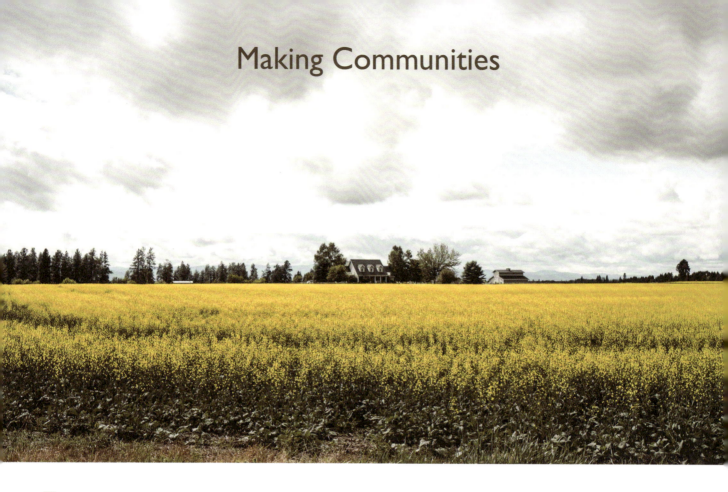

The Montana makers I met in the course of creating this book embody the power of a sense of place. Not only what they make, but how they make it is greatly influenced by their home. Montana has that kind of an impact: it is still so big, wild, beautiful, and largely empty of people, even in this day and age. The artists who have chosen to make their homes here love their place deeply and passionately, and that love is reflected in what they create.

After spending a few weeks with Montana makers, I felt the pull of this place and was ready to join their ranks. Although they are candid about the harsh winters, the sense of isolation, and the limited access to goods and services you're likely to find in larger, more populated locales, there's something about how they describe life in Montana that enthralls me. I imagine it's how people felt over two hundred years ago when Lewis and Clark returned from their expedition with tales of the grandeur and beauty of the West. Yes, there were hardships and sacrifices to be made, but that didn't stop thousands of pioneers from chasing the dream all the way to the Pacific Ocean.

So when I visited Steve Morley in his workshop, with its smell of cedar, puffs of sawdust in the air, and canoes in various stages of assembly in every nook and cranny, it was easy to set aside practical issues like lack of cell phone service and long, snowy winters when roads could become impassable, and instead focus on Steve's stories of summers spent plying the waters of Swan Lake in his handbuilt canoes, dodging bull moose when necessary; golden autumn months trail running with his kids along logging roads (always with bear spray at the ready!); and winters spent on the ski slopes of Whitefish. As we walked one of Steve's canoes across the road to Swan Lake, only a few hundred yards away, I was enraptured by tales of the wolverine who lived one winter under the deck of the log cabin that sat on the banks of the lake, and about how each of Steve's three children learned to kayak or canoe in a watercraft handbuilt just for them by their grandfather. Steve painted a picture of a life well-lived, a chance to create with his hands, build relationships with customers who shared his passion, and a home for his family that brought him joy and satisfaction.

Jess Neeley and Siri Larsen told similar tales of houses built from scratch and families raised with a deep connection to the natural world around them. It brought to mind Richard Louv's book *Last Child in the Woods: Saving our Children from Nature Deficit Disorder,* in which the author warns of the dangers of each succeeding generation of children losing touch with the natural world available in their own backyards:

"Within the space of a few decades, the way children understand and experience nature has changed radically. The polarity of the relationship has reversed. Today, kids are aware of the global threats to the environment—but their physical contact, their intimacy with nature, is fading . . . A kid today can likely tell you about the Amazon rain forest—but not about the last time he or she explored the woods in solitude, or lay in a field listening to the wind and watching the clouds move . . . This book explores the increasing divide between the young and the natural world, and the environmental, social, psychological, and spiritual implications of that change." Yet in Montana, that connection seems alive and well, and greatly valued by the people who make their homes there.

The influence of place is so strong for these makers that what they create is literally entwined with the land. Meghan Purcell's large-scale fiber panels are inspired by Montana mountain ranges and are created from the wool of local Icelandic sheep. Through her art, Meghan represents both the beauty and fragility of ranch life in Montana. Stella Moss is using her small home-based bakery to create a local supply chain that will link Montana farmers to local grain cleaners and mills, and ultimately to local farmers markets and those who love good bread and care about how it's made. And every aspect of The Farmers Daughter Fiber yarn company is place-based, from its very conception to its color inspirations to the names that dyer Candice English selects for the yarn bases and colors. Candice, a native Montanan whose heritage represents both the Blackfeet tribe and the white ranchers who settled here, explains that life in Montana is about finding a slower pace and room to enjoy and appreciate what nature has to offer, and she works to convey that through the nostalgic qualities imbued in her yarns.

If there is any maker who is the poster child for a Montana life, it would be Siri Larsen. The family homestead, built from the ground up by Siri's husband Chris Neill, is tucked into a bucolic corner of northwestern Montana, near the Canadian border. Every aspect of the family's life comes from their land and their own hands: Siri raises a small flock of sheep, shears and processes the wool, dyes it with botanical dyes she grows and forages, and then spins, knits, and weaves with the yarn. Chris, a self-taught craft brewer, opened HA Brewing in a refurbished outbuilding on the homestead, and the family has slowly built a microbrewery, taproom, and restaurant that draws both local community and tourists from miles around. Chatting with Siri over cold glasses of HA Brewing Summer Saison and Pioneer Pale on a mild summer afternoon, admiring the view all the way to the peaks of Glacier National Park, and listening to the sheep bleating in the nearby pasture, it is all but impossible not to imagine a life like this. Hard work and cold winters, yes, but so much beauty and joy, such a feeling of connection to the land, so many opportunities to spend your life outdoors in the fields, rivers, woods, and mountains, where the land feels almost untouched . . . a life well-lived, to be sure.

On the Farm: Montana Wool Works

In many ways, Siri Larsen is living the iconic Montana life: A homestead in a lush valley with mountain peaks on the horizon and a bubbling creek nearby. A small herd of sheep that Siri raises, shears, washes and handspins the wool, tints it with natural dyes, and then uses the yarn to knit or weave. A family home that Siri's husband Chris Neill built himself. And now, a brewery and restaurant right on the homestead that is housed in restored outbuildings, stocked with microbrews that Chris brews himself. Siri and her family have created the ultimate expression of living off the land, and in doing so, have fostered a local community in the small town of Eureka.

The sheep on Siri's farm are Gotland/BFL crosses, and Siri completes every step of creating sheep-to-needle yarn on her farm by hand. After shearing, the wool is skirted, washed, mordanted, and then dyed with natural dyes created from plants that Siri collects on and around the farm. The next steps are picking and then carding with an old drum carder and a Pat Green electric triple-carder on long-term loan. Finally, Siri spins the roving on Schacht Matchless and Ladybug spinning wheels.

Siri's fascination with yarn and knitting dates back to early childhood, when her Norwegian mother handed her a skein of wool and straight needles and taught her to knit. She paired this love of knitting with an obsession for natural dyes that began in college when she took a batik class. Siri fell in love with the process, but not the toxic chemicals that they were using. "I remember going to the library and looking up books on dyeing and batik. I pulled this book about natural dyeing off the shelf, and

that was it. I remember sitting there and thinking, this is incredible, I can't believe this is something people do! The book was out of print, so I photocopied the whole thing right there at the library and bound it." Although Siri didn't know much about plants at the time, she set her mind to learning, and now she grows and forages her own dye plants, including goldenrod, Queen Anne's lace, native purple beebalm, tansies, yarrow, and even mushrooms. She's started an indigo vat, as well, and indigo seedlings sit on her porch, waiting to be transplanted.

Right now, though, the focus is on the H.A. taproom, including the addition of a restaurant (up to this point, a food cart has served meals to visitors). The brewery's motto is "Brewed in Good Cheer!" and Siri explains that part of the experience they want to provide is serving fresh, local and delicious food. "We want to make a living, provide employment, serve good food, good beer, and good company," she smiles. And the brewery, housed in an open and spacious barn with picnic table seating spilling outdoors into the garden, does just that. It is cheerful and family-friendly, with the day's craft beers written on a chalkboard menu and breathtaking views from the outdoor beer garden. Every bit of the work is done by Chris and his crew, including canning and hand-bottling.

Behind the brewery sits the family home, which includes a bright, sunny crafting room for Siri to knit and weave in; a dyeing kitchen, with bottles of dried flowers stacked high on the shelves; and even a butchery, where Chris hand-crafts charcuterie from pigs raised on the farm. Numerous outbuildings, barns, and fenced pastures dot the surrounding landscape, and on many afternoons, the storm clouds roll in over the mountains in the distance. The family's livestock guardian dog posts himself in the sheep pasture, keeping a watchful eye on his flock. Siri rattles through a list of tasks to be completed that day, and it is clear that while the work is neverending, so is her joy in having carved out a life for herself and her family in this small corner of Big Sky country.

Montana Wool Works

Yarn Maker: Siri Larsen
Website: montanawoolworks.com
Instagram: montanawoolworks

H.A. Brewing Co.

Brewmaster: Chris Neill
Address: 2525 Grave Creek Rd., Eureka
Website: habrewing.com
Instagram: habrewing

Wooden Watercraft: Morley Canoes

When Greg Morley founded Morley Canoes in 1972, hand building watercraft was the only way to achieve both aesthetic beauty and top performance. "When my dad starting doing this," Steve Morley explains, "mass-produced boats couldn't rival the performance of handbuilt. You could have a boat that was really durable in the river, but the materials used meant that performance suffered. Our boats had the ability to perform well and look great, and building them by hand was the only way you could do it. The hand-built boats would out-perform the mass-produced boats every time." However, Steve says, "things have a changed a lot in the last five to eight years. You can mass-produce good performance and good appearance now."

Yet Steve notes that there are still many people who value hand-built watercraft for other reasons. "Our market has definitely changed. Now it's people looking for something that's hand-crafted and the story behind it. They come into the shop and there's something about someone building something for you. There's definitely something about a boat being handmade that inspires the person who will be using it and relying upon it."

The watercraft created by Morley Canoes are the ultimate expression of the love, care, and artistry that goes into building by hand. Every step of the process is handbuilt, using knowledge and skill acquired over the almost fifty years since Greg founded the company. Even the two 19th-century jigsaws in the Morley workshop are hand-powered (or in this case, foot-powered by a pedal that turns a belt, which in turn runs the saw blade up and down). A canoe's life begins when Steve travels to Washington to hand-pick Western

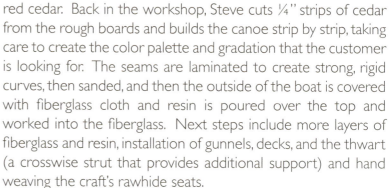

red cedar. Back in the workshop, Steve cuts ¼" strips of cedar from the rough boards and builds the canoe strip by strip, taking care to create the color palette and gradation that the customer is looking for. The seams are laminated to create strong, rigid curves, then sanded, and then the outside of the boat is covered with fiberglass cloth and resin is poured over the top and worked into the fiberglass. Next steps include more layers of fiberglass and resin, installation of gunnels, decks, and the thwart (a crosswise strut that provides additional support) and hand weaving the craft's rawhide seats.

In addition to a variety of canoe sizes and shapes, including a pack canoe that can be made as light as 14 pounds, Steve and his father build kayaks, paddleboards, and skiffs. In the front of the workshop sits a rowboat designed for the Glacier Park Boat Company, used as the model for tour boats on Lake McDonald. The Morleys hand carve oars, as well, shaping each set for the particular type of boat and the purpose for which it will be used.

Before working with his dad, Steve spent years windsurfing and canoe racing in Hawaii, which gave him an opportunity to experience the role that the canoe played in Polynesian culture. "The Polynesians understand their heritage. They're surrounded by it – the ocean is all around them. Here, as soon as the horses and white settlers came in, the canoes disappeared. Now the few authentic canoes left are only in museums." Greg has delved deeply into the Native American canoe culture, using historical documents to recreate designs lost to time and working with western tribes to help them rediscover how to build some of those designs.

Many of the customers who purchase Morley Canoes find the shop as they're driving by on the highway that curves along the eastern shore of Swan Lake. Steve is able to build only twelve boats a year, and there is a one to two-year wait list at any given time. "We could hire more people and start popping out boats faster," Steve reflects, "but my dad is really opposed to that. He wants to keep our work small-scale and personalized." Steve notes that "when you've got a lot of time invested in one piece, you get to know the person you're building for. I think about how they're going to use the boat, and when they come to pick it up, you see the satisfaction on their faces. When you're all done, it's really rewarding to look at something that started out as a stack of lumber that you crafted into something that people really appreciate."

Morley Canoes

Builders: Greg and Steve Morley

Address: 22030 Hwy 83N, Swan Lake

E-mail: morleycanoes.com

Phone: (406) 886-2242

Big Sky Ruana
by Andrea Hungerford

A ruana is an ingeniously shaped free-flowing poncho wrap, made from a single piece of fabric, with an open front. It is basically a blanket that you can wear! I love the simplicity of the structure, and how it so quickly and easily adds polish and style to whatever I'm wearing. I designed a Montana-style motif for the edges of this ruana to give it some visual interest, western flair, and a chance for the knitter to play with different color combinations.

FINISHED MEASUREMENTS
33.5 (48.75)" wide at back hem, and 28 (29)" long from shoulder.

MATERIALS
The Farmers Daughter Fibers Pishkun (100% Rambouillet wool; 255 yds/100 g)
MC: 5 (12) skeins in Antler Bone (1275 yds, plus an add'l 50 yds for fringe)
CC: 1 (2) skein(s) in Ranc Bronc (255 yds, plus an add'l 50 yds for fringe)

US 9 (5.5 mm) 24" or 32" circular needles
Stitch markers, stitch holders or waste yarn, tapestry needle

GAUGE
16 sts and 24 rows = 4" in stockinette stitch, blocked.

NOTES
The fronts of the Ruana are worked from the bottom up, starting with a garter stitch mosaic section and then continuing in Stockinette stitch. Stitches are then cast on for the neck and the back is knit from the top down, ending with a matching garter stitch mosaic section. To finish, stitches are picked up along edges and immediately bound off to prevent rolling.

DIRECTIONS
Right Front
Cast on 67 (99) sts in MC.

Work 4 rows in Garter stitch.
Next row (RS): K2, pm, work first row of chart, working bordered repeat 1 (2) time(s) to last 2 sts, pm, k2.
Note: Continue working 2 garter sts on each end every row, using whichever color you finished the previous row with.

Work chart one time.
Continue working in MC until Right Front measures 25" from CO edge, ending with a WS row.

Neck Shaping
Row 1 (RS): K2, ssk, K to end (1 st dec'd).
Row 2 (WS): K2, purl to last 2 sts, K2.
Rep these last two rows twice more. 64 (96) sts.
Row 7: K2, ssk, knit to end (1 st dec'd).
Row 8: K2, purl to last 4 sts, p2tog, k2 (1 st dec'd).
Rep these last two rows 4 (6) more times. 54 (82) sts.
Rep Rows 1 & 2 once (twice) more. 53 (80) sts.
Cut yarn and place on stitch holder.

Left Front
Work as for Right Front until Neck Shaping.

Neck Shaping
Row 1 (RS): K to last 4 sts, k2tog, k2 (1 st dec'd).
Row 2 (WS): K2, purl to last 2 sts, K2.
Rep these last two rows twice more. 64 (96) sts.
Row 7: K to last 4 sts, k2tog, k2 (1 st dec'd).
Row 8: K2, ssp, purl to last 2 sts, k2 (1 st dec'd).
Rep these last two rows 4 (6) more times. 54 (82) sts.
Rep Rows 1 & 2 once (twice) more. 53 (80) sts.

Next row (RS): Knit across Left Front, CO 28 (30) sts, return held Right Front sts to ndls and knit across Right Front. 134 (190) sts.
Work in St st until back measures 23.5 (24.5)" from back neck cast-on.

Smaller Size Only:
Next RS row: (K32, k2tog) 3 times, knit to end. 131 sts.

Larger Size Only:
Next RS row: K31, M1, (k32, m1) r times, knit to end. 195 sts.

Both Sizes:
Work 1 more row in St st.
Begin chart, working bordered repeat 3 (5) times while maintaining a 2-st Garter stitch border on each end, as for fronts.

Knit 4 rows of Garter st in MC.
BO all sts.
Wet block to measurements.

FINISHING
Starting at bottom of outer Left Front with RS facing, pick up and knit 1 st for every 2 rows, to the edge of the back bottom. Knit one row. BO knitwise loosely to keep edges from pulling too tight or puckering. Repeat on Right Front side, and then again around the inside edge of Right Front, up around the neck, and down the inner edge of Left Front.

Weave in all ends and steam block.

FRINGE
Cut 38 sets of MC and CC (12" lengths) for Right Front.
Cut 38 sets of MC and CC (12" lengths) for Left Front.
Cut 68 sets of MC and CC (12" lengths) for Back.

Grasp each set of two strands in the middle and fold in half, then thread the folded piece through a tapestry needle. Starting on one end, thread through the bound-off end of Right Front from front to back, creating a loop. Thread the loose ends through the loop and pull gently (not too tight). Continue across the bound-off end, evenly spacing the 38 sets of fringe. Repeat for Left Front and Back. Trim if desired.

Reclaimed Art Inspired by Nature: Ruby & Revolver

Ruby & Revolver's rugged, Western aesthetic echoes throughout Jess Neeley's workshop, tucked high in the forested slopes of the Bitterroot Valley. The metals and stones she uses – primarily jasper and turquoise – similarly echo Montana's long history of mining and its reliance on minerals pulled from the ground. But Jess brings her own sensibilities to her work, fashioning many of her jewelry pieces to reflect the natural world around her, and focusing on sustainability and minimal impact by using reclaimed metals and stones. "Reclaimed art. Inspired by nature. Made with heart + soul," is Ruby & Revolver's tagline.

"I've always been drawn to earthy colors," Jess reflects, "things that I see in my natural environment. I try to be mindful now about where I buy and where it comes from. I always knew that I wanted to work with reclaimed metal, and that changed my trajectory. My work isn't ever going to be a high-finish product. I'll always be working with a limited quantity, materials that can't be made into anything and everything. I had to own that and take that reality into consideration."

Growing up, Jess was exposed to her father's work as a metalsmith, but her jewelry-making skills are completely self-taught. And using reclaimed metal adds time and difficulty to her work, because the metal has to be melted down first. "I often don't know the life the metal has lived before," she explains. "It's easy to burn your metal and make mistakes – it's kind of finicky. But I love the history of reclaimed metal; some pieces I just have to keep a portion of them in their true form, like the handle of a spoon, or the maker's mark."

The process also involves toxic and dangerous chemicals, and a mask, gloves, and a commercial venting system are necessary safety components. Once the metal is melted into liquid form, Jess presses it into sheet metal or wire to create her base material. Next, she sketches a design concept, creates a bezel for the stone, and then begins to build the piece, one level of soldering at a time. "It's really satisfying when I picture something in my head and it comes to fruition. I like the transformation from a three-dimensional object that inspires me or something I picture in my head, to a finished piece."

But the pieces don't always come out as Jess would like, and it's a slow process – sometimes she spends an entire day creating one ring. And, once Jess' daughter Indy was born, she had to fight even harder to find balance. Right now, her priority is being with Indy and her husband Kyle, taking time to go backpacking, pick wild roses, ride bikes, and hang out in the hammock in the evenings. Jess' ability to balance work and family is challenged by the great demand for her pieces. They regularly sell out in under five minutes after she posts an update on her online store, and she receives so many inquiries and e-mails that she's had to implement an auto response, letting people know that she likely won't have time to answer. This kind of a hue and cry for her work could have pushed Jess to work harder and longer, find ways to increase and modernize her production. Instead, Jess has fought to stay true to the pace and process that feels right to her. "I've really had to let go and just hope that people who love my work will still be there."

Right now, aside from online sales, Ruby & Revolver is available at only one show a year, hosted by the Montgomery Distillery in Missoula. But Ruby & Revolver may soon take its act on the road, so to speak. Her family's forced evacuation from their home last year due to nearby forest fires got Jess thinking about how to plan ahead for fire danger, and out of this necessity was born the concept of a mobile studio. The idea is for the family of three to travel and work, allowing Jess to continue designing and see some of the country at the same time. "I'd like to have Kyle come with me. He's highly organized and a beautiful artist in his own right," she says. In this way, prioritizing time with family and time in nature, Jess feels that she will be able to keep doing what she calls "my most honest work."

Ruby & Revolver

Artist: Jess Neeley

Website: rubyandrevolver.com

Instagram: rubyandrevolver

Castilleja Wrap

by Shellie Anderson

Castilleja is the scientific name for Indian Paintbrush, one of the wildflowers found along hiking trails in the mountains of Montana, and a close match to beautiful orange-red hue of this versatile, unisex wrap.

FINISHED MEASUREMENTS
18.5" width x 60.5" length

MATERIALS
The Farmers Daughter Fibers Juicy DK (100% wool; 274 yds/100 g); 4 skeins in color Pretty Shield
US 6 (4 mm) needles
Stitch markers, tapestry needle

GAUGE
22 sts and 28 rows = 4" in stockinette stitch,

NOTES
This is a generously sized reversible unisex wrap. The wrap features garter edgings, bands of stockinette stitch, diagonal rib and a diamond motif.

STITCH PATTERNS
Chart A is worked flat over a multiple of 6 sts.
Chart B is worked flat over a multiple of 12 sts.

DIRECTIONS
CO 102 sts.
Row 1 (WS): K3 sts, pm, k to 3 sts before end of row, pm.
Knit 4 more rows.

Stitch Pattern Sequence
Note: Work the 3 edge sts at either end of each row in garter stitch. End each pattern sequence with a WS row.

CHART A - work for 5.5" -
(approx 3 pattern repeats)
Stockinette Stitch - work for 2.5"

CHART B - work for 5.5" -
(approx 3 pattern repeats)
Stockinette Stitch - work for 4"

CHART A - work for 5.5"
Stockinette Stitch - work for 4"

CHART A - work for 5.5"
Stockinette Stitch - work for 4"

CHART A - work for 5.5"
Stockinette Stitch - work for 4"

CHART B - work for 5.5"
Stockinette Stitch - work for 2.5"

CHART A - work for 5.5"

Knit 6 rows.
BO all sts loosely.

FINISHING
Block to measurements.
Weave in ends.

Chart A

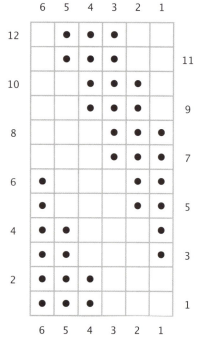

Chart B

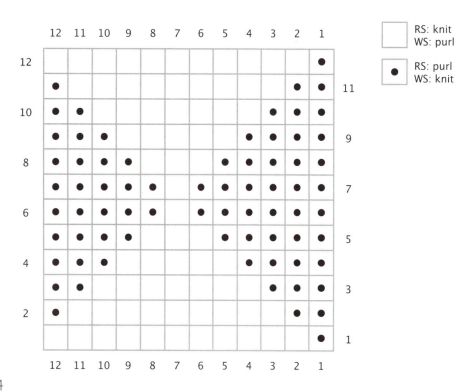

Pebble Shore Beanie

by Renate Yerkes / Elephino PDX

This unisex hat is designed to accentuate the woolly nature of this yarn. Its beautiful textured appearance is equally flattering on men and women, and is fully reversible. The clever construction creates a clean, finished look and a refreshing opportunity to knit a hat from the top down!

FINISHED MEASUREMENTS
For adult head measurements ranging between 20-22.5"
Hat circumference: 16" (40.6 cm)
Unstretched height from crown to rim, unfolded: approx. 12" (30.5 cm), after blocking; with folded rim: approx. 8.5" (21.6 cm)

MATERIALS
Thirteen Mile Yarns (100% Organic Wool; 215 yds/100 g); 1 skein in color Brown Heather
US 6 (4 mm) 16" circular, US 5 (3.75 mm) 16" circular, and US 6 (4 mm) DPNs
Stitch marker, tapestry needle

GAUGE
25 stitches x 32 rows = 4" (10 cm) in Broken Rib pattern on US 6 (4 mm) needles, after blocking.

NOTES
Similar in construction to 'toe-up' sock knitting, this hat is cast on at the crown using Judy's Magic Cast-on method, then finished using the sewn cast-off method at the bottom hem. It is worked on the "knit" side in the round but is fully reversible when complete.

Recommended tutorials (available on youtube.com):
For the best cast-on method, see *How to Do Judy's Magic Cast-on Using Double Pointed Needles*, by Nancy Wynn
For t he preferred sewn bind-off (in the round) method, see *KNITFreedom - Invisible Ribbed Bind-Off - A Stretchy Invisible Bind-Off for 1x1 Ribbing*, by KNITFreedom

For ease of instructions, DPNs with sts on them will be referred to in order as DPN 1, DPN 2, DPN 3 & DPN 4, with the separate needle referred to as the working DPN.

STITCH PATTERNS
Broken Rib stitch pattern (knit side):
Rnd 1: K1, p1.
Rnd 2: Knit.
Rep rnds 1 and 2.

Reverse Broken Rib stitch pattern (purl side):
Rnd 1: K1, p1.
Rnd 2: Purl.
Rep rnds 1 and 2.

DIRECTIONS
Beginning at the Crown
With US 6 (4 mm) DPNs, using Judy's Magic Cast-on method (refer to recommended tutorial if needed), cast on 18 sts alternately on top and bottom DPNs, plus one extra st on the top DPN (DPN 1). There are 37 sts in total, with 19 on the top DPN (DPN 1) and 18 sts on the bottom DPN (DPN 2). Tie off with a double knot after last cast-on stitch to prevent unraveling. Without turning work over, move DPNs to left hand, rotating them 180° so that working tips are now facing to the right. DPN 2 (the one with 18 sts on it) will now be the top DPN (becoming DPN 1 in next round).

Round 1 (set-up round): With new working DPN, working sts from DPN 1, [k1, p1] x 4, k2tog (1 st dec), p1, [k1, p1] x 3, k1fb (1 st inc). 18 sts on 1st worked DPN. Without turning work over, move DPNs to left hand, rotating them 180° and sliding sts on DPN 2 (now positioned on top) down to working tip. With new working DPN, k1fb (1 st inc); this needle now becomes DPN 2 (2 sts).

With new working DPN, [k1, p1] x 8, k1fb x 2 (2 st inc); this needle now becomes DPN 3. Next, slip last 3 sts from DPN 3 onto new working needle; this new needle now becomes DPN 4. 17 sts on DPN 3 and 3 sts on DPN 4 There are now 40 sts altogether on the four DPNs.

Round 2: With new working DPN, working sts from DPN 1; k17, slip remaining stitch from DPN 1 onto DPN 2, bringing st count to 3 on DPN 2 (17 sts on DPN 1).

DPN 2: K1fb × 2, k1 (5 sts).
DPN 3: Knit (17 sts).
DPN 4: K1fb × 2, k1 (5 sts).

Round 3: DPNs 1 & 3: [K1, p1] × 8, k1 (17 sts each).
DPNs 2 & 4: P1, k1fb × 2, k1, p1 (7 sts each).

Round 4: DPNs 1 & 3: Knit (17 sts each).
DPNs 2 & 4: K2, k1fb × 2, k3 (9 sts each).

Round 5: DPNs 1 & 3: [K1, p1] × 8, k1 (17 sts each).
DPNs 2 & 4: P1, k1, p1, k1fb × 2, [k1, p1] × 2 (11 sts each).

Round 6: DPNs 1 & 3: Knit (17 sts each).
DPNs 2 & 4: K4, k1fb × 2, k5. (13 sts each).

Round 7: DPNs 1 & 3: [K1, p1] × 8, k1 (17 sts each).
DPNs 2 & 4: [P1, k1] × 2, p1, k1fb × 2, [k1, p1] × 3 (15 sts each).

Round 8: DPNs 1 & 3: Knit (17 sts each).
DPNs 2 & 4: K6, k1fb × 2, k7 (17 sts each).

Round 9: DPNs 1 & 3: [K1, p1] × 8, k1 (17 sts each).
DPNs 2 & 4: [P1, k1] × 3, p1, k1fb × 2, [k1, p1] × 4 (19 sts each).

Round 10: DPNs 1 & 3: Knit (17 sts each).
DPNs 2 & 4: K8, k1fb × 2, k9 (21 sts each).

Round 11: DPNs 1 & 3: [K1, p1] × 8, k1 (17 sts each).
DPNs 2 & 4: [P1, k1] × 4, p1, k1fb × 2, [k1, p1] × 5 (23 sts each).

Round 12: DPNs 1 & 3: Knit (17 sts each).
DPNs 2 & 4: K10, k1fb × 2, k11 (25 sts each).

Round 13: DPNs 1 & 3: [K1, p1] × 8, k1 (17 sts each).
DPNs 2 & 4: [P1, k1] × 5, p1, k1fb × 2, [k1, p1] × 6 (27 sts each).

Round 14: DPNs 1 & 3: Knit (17 sts each).
DPNs 2 & 4: K12, k1fb × 2, k13 (29 sts each).

Round 15: DPNs 1 & 3: [K1, p1] × 8, k1 (17 sts each).
DPNs 2 & 4: [P1, k1] × 6, p1, k1fb × 2, [k1, p1] × 7 (31 sts each),

Round 16: DPNs 1 & 3: Knit (17 sts each).
DPNs 2 & 4: K14, k1fb x 2, k15 (33 sts each).

There are now a total of 100 sts altogether.

Next Round: Switching to US 6 (4 mm) 16" circular needles, continue to work hat in Broken Rib pattern (refer to Stitch Patterns) and place marker at start of round once DPNs have been replaced.

Continue to knit in Broken Rib stitch pattern, slipping marker as you come to it in subsequent rounds, until hat measures 7" (17.75 cm) from crown, completing last round to marker.

Next Round: Switching to US 5 (3.75 mm) 16" circular needles, continue in Broken Rib stitch pattern until hat measures 8" (20.33 cm) from crown, completing with round 2 of stitch pattern.

Next round: Begin to use the Reverse Broken Rib stitch pattern (refer to Stitch Patterns), continuing in this pattern until hat measures 10.5" (26.66 cm) from crown, completing last round to marker.

Next Round: Switching back to US 6 (4 mm) 16" circular needles, continue in Reverse Broken Rib stitch pattern until hat measures 11.5" (29.25 cm) from crown and completing with round 1 of stitch pattern.

Cut yarn, leaving about a 60" (150 cm) tail.

FINISHING
With tapestry needle, bind off hat brim with the sewn or "invisible" bind-off method (refer to recommended tutorial if needed). Weave in ends. To block, soak hat in lukewarm water and gently squeeze out excess moisture, being careful not to wring. Lay flat to measurements (8" (20.33 cm) in width, 12" (30.5 cm) in height) and let dry.

Catcus Blossom Collective in Livingston (above left and right), and Bozeman's Genuine Ice Cream Co. (below)

Street scenes in Bozeman (right), Fleur Bake Shop in Whitefish (below left), and Kalispell's farmers market (below right)

Around Montana

Felted Wool Artistry: Meghan Purcell

Raw Icelandic wool is the inspiration, the material, and the underlying message of Meghan Purcell's large-scale pieces. Although Meghan has a background in fine arts, she had never experimented with fiber until she saw a stand at the local farmers market. The woman there "had all of these bags of wool in different natural colors that struck me to the core," she recalls. Meghan reached out to the woman, who turned out to be Barb Gunness of Wolf Ridge Icelandics, and a long-standing relationship was formed.

In the beginning, Meghan had no idea what she was going to do with the wool, but she felt driven to use it in a way that brought visual life to Montana's landscapes and the state's history and tradition of ranching. "My work speaks to this region," she explains. "It's very reflective of the crucial role that agriculture and animal husbandry plays here." Using only undyed wool, including the wide range of natural colors from Icelandic sheep, Meghan draws inspiration from the shape and line of Montana's mountains, valleys, and plains. She begins with the branch that the piece will hang from – often found already smoothed and shaped by the flow of a nearby river – and spreads the wool out in layers. Once she is satisfied with the entire composition, she applies soap and water to the surface, agitating the wool continuously to cause it to felt. The piece is then hung to dry.

Meghan's raw, textural pieces bring to life Montana's identity in landscape and ranch heritage. "I'm motivated by the process and the relationship to the farmers – the connections I make through art," she elaborates. Each of the steps in her process is intentional, from selecting 100% locally-sourced wool, to periodically assisting with the sheep shearing and forming relationships with ranches that use sustainable practices.

One of Meghan's recent exhibitions was titled "Behind the Wool: Honoring the Integrity of Sheep Ranchers." The exhibited work was a collaboration with six local farmers, and each piece was constructed from an individual farm's wool. The result was a visual representation of each farm's deep pride in and dedication to its flock, and of Meghan's efforts to investigate and understand the challenges and struggles that modern-day ranchers face in attempting to preserve and sustain sheep ranching in Montana.

Recently, Meghan has began to enclose her work in frames, creating the appearance of a three-dimensional painting. The presentation "elevates the fiber medium to art," she reflects. "It takes it to a different level." Meaghan expresses an interest in continuing to push the fiber medium from a craft to fine art. Her work is currently exhibited in galleries and sold on commission through her website, and she is in the process of creating an installation for a new boutique hotel in Bozeman. All of these venues give Meghan an opportunity to speak for Montana's farms and ranches through her work. "I think a lot of Montanans are proud of our open lands and our ranch culture – those go hand in hand. We like it wild here. There are a lot of really important issues we're facing today to preserve that open, wild land. Being able to help these ranches stay open and contribute to this community is what inspires and drives me."

Meghan Purcell Art

Website: meghanpurcell.com

Instagram: meghanpurcellart

Exhibition: Old Main Gallery, Bozeman

Pendleton Buckets

by Andrea Hungerford

I love projects that utilize small amounts of beautiful fabric, and the heavy weight of Pendleton wool allows you to easily create these versatile storage buckets. Beautiful enough to serve as decorative fixtures themselves, these buckets don't have to be hidden away; keep them out on display to stow yarns, fabrics, sewing supplies, hats and scarves, or just about anything else you can think of!

FINISHED DIMENSIONS
8.25" diameter, 26" circumference, 8.75" tall

MATERIALS
Fabric A: 2/3 yard of heavyweight microsuede, shown in color Espresso (Etsy.com/shop/topfabric)
Fabric B: 3/8 yard of Pendleton wool
1 yard of craft fuse interfacing
Size 16 denim sewing machine needle
Matching thread
Optional: small square of leather

CUTTING

From Fabric A, cut:
* One 9" diameter circle (bottom lining)
* One 8 ¾ x 30" rectangle (bucket lining)
* One 9 ¼" diameter circle (bucket bottom)
* One 3" x 28" rectangle (top rim - you can make your rim wider if you'd like)

From Fabric B, cut:
* One 8 ¾" x 30" rectangle (bucket exterior)

From interfacing, cut:
* One 9" diameter circle
* One 8 ¾ x 30" rectangle

CONSTRUCTION

1. Fuse interfacing circle and rectangle to wrong sides of lining circle and rectangle.

2. With right sides together and using a 1/2" seam allowance, stitch the lining rectangle to the lining circle, leaving a 1" overlap at the beginning and stitching right up to the first stitch, so there's no gap (this is called the "pinch point"). Backstitch at beginning and end. You should have overlap leftover at the end, as well. No need to pin--it works better to adjust as you go along, easing with your fingers and correcting the position as you go. *Figure 1.*

3. Line up the ends of the rectangle in parallel, right sides together, and pin. Draw a line from top to bottom, ending at the pinch point, to ensure a straight seam. Stitch from the top along the line to the pinch point, then backstitch. *Figure 2.* Trim seam to 1/2" and press open.

4. Repeat Steps 2 & 3 with the exterior circle and Fabric B rectangle.

5. Turn the exterior right side out, but do not turn out the lining. Pop the lining into the exterior bag, wrong sides together, aligning seams. Pin, then baste around opening, 1/2" from edge. *Figure 3.* If liner is too big, pull it out and stitch another side seam 1/4" in from the original seam. If liner and exterior are not the same height, trim the edges before basting.

6. Fit the rim inside the opening of the bag, leaving 1/2" or more overlap at beginning and end.

Seam short ends together to form a ring, then trim seam to 1/2". Press seam open. Fold and press the long edges 1/2" to the wrong side. *Figure 4.*

7. Pin the rim inside the bag, right side of ring facing right side of lining, aligning seams and raw edges. Stitch on the fold line, 1/2" from the edge. *Figure 5.* Press seam toward the rim.

8. Flip the rim up and fold to the right side of the bag. Pin in place, aligning seam and making sure that the pressed-under edge stays tucked under. Starting at the seam, edgestitch around the rim. *Figure 6.*

9. Shape and finger-press the bag. Press top rim.

10. Optional: cut a small rectangle of leather, hand-stamp or burn in a logo or lettering, and affix to the top of the bag with two rivets. See klumhouse.com/blog/rivets for a rivet-setting tutorial.

Bags for Adventure: Western Bound Goods

With no sewing experience and only two bag-making classes under her belt, Jill Johnson set up her sewing machine in her parents' basement and began what would grow into Western Bound Goods. The style she eventually settled on combines Pendleton wool's Native American-inspired prints with rugged waxed canvas and leather accents. The bags look equally at home in the city or the country, carrying a laptop or everything needed for a day hike. The classic rolltop backpack, weekender duffel, tote, satchel, and bucket bag all reflect Western Bound's tagline: "Inspired by the West. Created for all your Adventures."

Jill credits the years she lived in Portland, Oregon for igniting her creative spark, and the aesthetic of Montana for the bags' rustic, western look. "The bags are really a combination of my life experiences, living in Portland and Montana," she reflects. "I chose Pendleton because I'd been gifted a Pendleton blanket while in Portland, and I recognized the quality and beauty of the wool. The bags are not only made in the west, they embody the style of the west: rustic freedom, exploration, adventure. I think of them as inspired by what I have experienced in my life."

Jill makes every bag by hand in her Bozeman studio, located in an historic school building that is now the Emerson Center for the Arts & Culture. She sources her materials from American companies whenever possible, including the waxed canvas, vegetable tanned leather, and Pendleton wool. The materials are chosen for their durability, and Western Bound bags are made to last. Jill notes that one of the factors that draws her to leather and waxed canvas is that it only looks better as it is ages, weathers, and is put to use.

Western Bound bags are sold online, at galleries and stores, and in-person at handcraft shows that Jill attends throughout the year. "The bag materials are very tactile, and people want to touch them," she comments. As a result, Jill often has the opportunity to get into discussions with her customers and share with them the importance of supporting local makers. She values that connection between the maker and consumer, and believes that it opens the way for people to build understanding and appreciation for what goes into making a quality product.

"I never even thought of myself as a creative person," Jill confesses, "but I kept wanting to learn more and more about the different ways to make a bag, how to work with leather, and the materials I could use. It was just that energy and passion that pushed me in this direction."

Western Bound Goods

Designer and Sewist: Jill Johnson

Website: westernboundgoods.com

Esty: etsy.com/shop/westernboundgoods

Instgram: western_bound_goods

Candice Cardigan

by Kjerste Whaley

SIZES
Women's S (M, L, XL)
Approx chest measurement 32 (38, 44, 50, 61, 66)"
Shown in Size S with approx ± 6–9" ease

FINISHED MEASUREMENTS
Chest Circumference: 38 (44, 50, 56, 65, 70)"
Back Length: 26 (28, 30, 30, 32, 32)"

MATERIALS
The Farmers Daughter Foxy Lady (70% Superwash Merino /30% Silk; 428 yds / 100 g), 2 (2, 3, 3, 3, 3) skeins in Sam Elliot
The Farmers Daughter Mighty Mo (70% Mohair /30% Silk; 459 yds / 50 g), 2 (2, 3, 3, 3, 3) skeins in Paul Newman
US 7 (4.5 mm) 40" circular needles
Tapestry needle

GAUGE
17 sts and 26 rows = 4" in stockinette stitch, with 1 strand of Foxy Lady held together with 1 strand of Might Mo, blocked

NOTES
Garment is knit flat lengthwise as a long rectangle. Short ends of the rectangle are then seamed, and the two joined long sides are seamed to create a loose shrug style cardigan.

DIRECTIONS
Using long-tail cast on method, CO 348 (382, 416, 442, 498, 528) sts.

Row 1 (WS): *K1, p1; rep from * to end.

Work 1×1 ribbing as established for 2.5", ending with a WS row.

Next Row (RS): Knit.
Next Row (WS): Purl.

Continue working in St st as established until piece measures 13 (14, 15, 15, 16, 16)" from CO edge. For longer length, work to 15 (16, 17, 17, 18, 18)", keeping in mind that each additional inch knit will add 2" to total back length and this may require additional yarn.

BO all sts loosely in pattern.

FINISHING
Block rectangle to measurements.

Fold in half, with right sides together, and seam the two short ends together using Mattress Stitch. Be careful not to pull too tightly causing puckers.

Lay garment flat with right sides together again, making sure seam is centered (shown as dashed line on sewing instructions) on the piece. Seam center of long side without ribbing, leaving 11 (11.5, 12, 12, 13, 13.5)" openings for the arms at either end. Weave in ends.

BLOCKING MEASUREMENTS

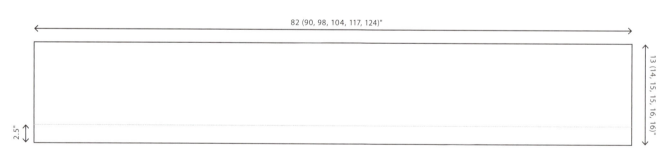

82 (90, 98, 104, 117, 124)"

13 (14, 15, 15, 16, 16)"

2.5"

SEWING INSTRUCTIONS

11 (11.5, 12, 12, 13, 13.5)"   18 (22, 25, 28, 32.5, 35)"   11 (11.5, 12, 12, 13, 13.5)"

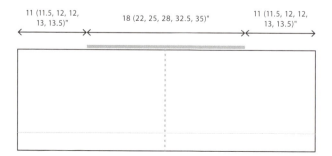

Hand Dyed: The Farmers Daughter Fibers

The role of place is paramount in the inspiration, design, and realization of The Farmers Daughter Fibers. "Our yarns are inspired by my Blackfoot heritage and Montana roots," says owner and founder Candice English. Born to a Native American mother and a white rancher father, Candice understands first-hand many of Montana's dualities: wilderness and cultivated farmland, freedom and long-standing tradition, Native American and white settler. Candice brought all of these aspects to bear when she created Farmers Daughter. First and foremost, she wants the yarns she makes to embody the Montana way of life. "There is such a nostalgic feel to Montana and that was something I really wanted to put in our brand. We move at a slower pace here, and I think a lot of people want that. Through our brand, working with our yarns and fibers, hand crafters can realize a little of that feeling."

Three years ago, Candice was working a nine-to-five corporate job, with two kids, a white picket fence, and a lot of stress. "I didn't feel like I was living the life I was supposed to," she recalls, musing now that this was her mid-life crisis, coming along a little earlier than mid-life. "I had always wanted to be an artist – both my mom and sisters are – but I can't do any of the traditional fine arts, and never found something that was the right fit, until I started dyeing yarn. This was the first art that I had encountered that I was good at and it was very much a spiritual experience, too. I had a lot of healing to do and a lot of things to work through, and I did it all through Farmers Daughter. It allowed me to take the spiritual aspects of the land – Montana is such a big part of my life, and of Farmers Daughter. I have such a spiritual connection here, and I felt like I could embody that in the yarns I was dyeing."

Many of the Farmers Daughter yarns carry Blackfoot names, and Candice is excited about the opportunity to use her art to help educate others about Native American history. "It's a vulnerable thing for

me to go to that place – it's very personal, and I've had to develop enough confidence to say that my voice does matter in this forum. We have a lot of discussions about cultural appropriation, diversity, and inclusion, and about what contemporary Native American art looks like today. It's all part of trying to honor our heritage, while at the same time, staying relevant and fitting into the modern world."

Candice began selling her yarn at the local farmers market, and then at Made Montana, the biggest makers market in the state. "I took every single opportunity that was offered to me," she laughs. Then she moved on to bigger shows like the Gorge Fiber Festival, and she continued to grow from there. Last year, she held the first Montana Mountain retreat. "I wanted people to see Montana – it is so much of who we are as a brand, and I wanted to share that with people. And I really wanted to show people how to slow down and invoke this true Montana way of life." The retreat is held at the Izzak Walton Inn in Glacier National Park, and

Candice notes that the lack of technological connectivity available at the Inn plays a significant role in helping people find that relaxation.

One of Candice's greatest joys in the creation and growth of Farmers Daughter has been the fiber arts community. "I'm finding my own community in this group of women who really inspire me and lift me up; it's very fulfilling and it makes it easy to keep going . . . A part of our success is that the makers who would typically be considered our competition are our friends, instead. Our strength is in the relationships we've created." In the future, Candice hopes to work with Montana's sheep ranchers to explore using wool from other sheep breeds, and featuring Montana wool in Farmers Daughter yarns. And just as important is finding time to get away to the mountains for the weekend and enjoy time with her family. "I have all of these ideas, and as a result, I can get ahead of myself sometimes," she reflects. "It's important to look at what will really work and what will bring me joy over the long run."

The Farmers Daughter Fibers

Head Dyer: Candice English

Website: thefarmersdaughterfibers.com

Address: 210 17th St. N., Great Falls

Instagram: thefarmersdaughterfibers.com

Gallatin Wraparound

by Andrea Hungerford

I love how a simple rectangle with two slits for armholes magically turns into a beautifully draped wraparound cardigan! This piece is remarkably easy to knit, but it is dramatic and sophisticated when worn, the fringe adds a dash of flair, and it looks entirely different if you pull it across to button it, or leave it open. Tubular cast-on / cast-off and ribbing creates a polished edging. Because you knit it vertically, and then it drapes on a diagonal, playing with different colors and textures of yarns will yield strikingly different results. I love mixing yarn bases, and both of these versions experiment with combining different weights and textures of yarns. With two pattern variations at different gauges, you can combine an endless variety of yarns!

SIZES
Women's XS–S (M, L, XL, XXL)
Approx chest measurement 32–36 (38–42, 44–48, 50-54, 56-60)"
Shown in Size M with approx +4–9" ease with fronts closed

FINISHED MEASUREMENTS
Chest Circumference: 41.5 (49, 57, 65, 68)", with fronts open
Back Length: 33 (35.5, 37)"

NOTES
Cardigan is worked flat from the right front to the left front, starting and ending with 1×1 ribbing. Three strands of yarn are held together throughout: 2 strands of The Farmers Daughter Foxy Lady and 1 strand of The Farmers Daughter Mighty Mo.

THE FARMERS DAUGHTER FIBERS VERSION

MATERIALS
The Farmers Daughter Foxy Lady (70% Merino/30% silk; 428 yds / 100 g), 6 (6, 6, 7, 7) skeins in color Hill Country
The Farmers Daughter Mighty Mo (70% Mohair/30% silk; 459 yds / 50 g), 3 (3, 3, 4, 4) skeins in color Eagle Eye
US 8 (5 mm) 24" or 32" circular needles
US 8 (5 mm) DPNs or 12" circular needles (for sleeves)
Tapestry needle, stitch markers, 2 one-inch buttons

GAUGE
14 sts and 20 rows = 4" in stockinette stitch, blocked, with 2 strands of Foxy Lady held together with 1 strand of Mighty Mo

DIRECTIONS
Body
Use tubular cast-on to end up with 121 (129, 135, 137, 141) sts (see Techniques in Glossary for tubular cast-on).

Work 5 rows of tubular cast-on.

Continue working 1×1 rib as follows:
Row 1 (RS): Sl1 wyib, *p1, k1; rep from * to end.
Row 2 (WS): Sl1 wyib, *k1, p1; rep from * to end.

Rep rows 1 & 2 until piece measures 1" from CO edge, ending with a WS row.

Left Front
Row 1 (RS): Sl1 wyib, (p1, k1) 3 times, p1, knit to last 8 sts, (p1, k1) 4 times.
Row 2 (WS): Sl1 wyib, (k1, p1) 3 times, k1, purl to last 8 sts, (k1, p1) 4 times.
Row 3: Sl1 wyib, (p1, k1) 3 times, p1, knit to last 8 sts, p1, k1, bind off 2 sts, k1, p1, k1.
Row 4: Sl1 wyib, k1, p1, k1, CO 2sts using backwards loop or cable CO, purl to last 8 sts, (k1, p1) 4 times.

Rep rows 1 & 2 until Left Front measures 14 (17, 20, 23.5, 24.5)" from CO edge, ending with a WS row.

Armholes
Next row (RS): Sl1 wyib, (p1, k1) 3 times, p1, k63 (66, 69, 69, 72), BO 28 (31, 34, 35, 35) sts (see Techniques in Glossary for binding off in the center of a row), knit to last 8 sts, (p1, k1) 4 times.
Next row (WS): Sl1 wyib, (k1, p1) 3 times, k1, p14 (16, 16, 17, 18), CO 28 (31, 34, 35, 35) sts using backwards loop or cable CO, purl to last 8 sts, (k1, p1) 4 times.

Continue working as established until Center Back measures 13.5 (15, 17, 18, 19)" from armhole BO, ending with a WS row.

Work second Armhole as described above.

Right Front
Continue working as established until Right Front measures 12.5 (15.5, 18.5, 22.25, 23.25)" from armhole BO, ending with a WS row.

Buttonhole
Next Row (RS): Sl1 wyib, (p1, k1) 3 times, p1, knit to last 8 sts, p1, k1, bind off 2 sts, k1, p1, k1.
Next Row (WS): Sl1 wyib, k1, p1, k1, CO 2 sts using backwards loop or cable CO, purl to last 8 sts, (k1, p1) 4 times.

Work 2 more rows as established. Then change to 1×1 rib as follows:
Row 1 (RS): Sl1 wyib, *p1, k1; rep from * to end.
Row 2 (WS): Sl1 wyib, *k1, p1; rep from * to end.
Rep rows 1 & 2 until piece measures 13.75 (16.75, 19.75, 23.25, 24.25)" from Armhole BO, ending with a WS row.

Set-up for Tubular BO as follows:
Row 1: *K1, sl1 wyif; rep from * to last st, k1.
Row 2: *Sl1 wyif, k1; rep from * to last st, sl1 wyif.
Work Tubular BO (see Techniques in Glossary).

Sleeves
Change to DPNs or 12" circulars and work the same for each Armhole.

With RS facing, starting at the underarm and pick up and knit one st in each BO off Armhole st, and then one st in each CO Armhole st. Join for working the rnd, placing m to mark BOR at underarm. 56 (62, 68, 70, 70) sts.

Shape sleeve cap as follows:
Row 1: K31 (35, 38, 38, 39), work GSR.
Row 2: P 5 (7, 7, 5, 7), work GSR.
Row 3: K to 2 sts past prev GSR, knitting ds together, work GSR.
Row 4: P to 2 sts past prev GSR, purling ds together, work GSR.
Rep last 2 rows 11 (13, 14, 14, 14) more times. Knit to end of rnd.

Cont working St st in the rnd until sleeve measures 4" from underarm.

Work dec rnd as follows:
Dec rnd: K1, k2tog, knit to last 3 sts, ssk, k1. 2 sts dec'd. 54 (60, 66, 68, 68) sts.

Rep dec rnd every 4th rnd 13 (15, 15, 16, 15) more times. Cont working in St st until sleeve measures 18 (18.5, 18.5, 19, 19)" along underarm (between decreases).

Twisted Rib Edging
Next rnd: *K1tbl, p1; rep from * to end of rnd.

Work twisted rib for 1.5". BO all sts in pattern, or use Tubular BO.

FINISHING
Block pieces to measurements. Add fringe on Left Front, if desired.

FRINGE
Cut 2 pieces of Foxy Lady and 2 pieces of Mighty Mo, each 10" long. Hold all 4 strands together and fold in half. Thread through tapestry needle, then thread through left front border, starting at far edge, from front to back. Pull ends through loop to knot. Repeat across the left front, spacing fringe 1" apart.

SHIBUI KNITS VERSION

MATERIALS

Shibui Knits Lunar (60% extra fine merino / 40% mulberry silk, 401 yds / 50 g), 4 (4, 5, 6. 7) skeins in color Ivory

Shibui Knits Twig (46% linen / 42% recycled silk / 12% wool; 190 yds / 50g), 8 (9, 11, 13, 14) skeins in color Caffeine

US 6 (4 mm) 24" or 32" circular needles

US 6 (4 mm) DPNs or 12" circular needles (for sleeves)

Tapestry needle, stitch markers, 2 one-inch buttons

GAUGE

19 sts and 25 rows = 4" in Stockinette stitch, blocked

DIRECTIONS

Body

Use tubular cast-on to end up with 161, (173, 181, 185, 191) sts (see Techniques in Glossary for tubular cast-on).

Continue working 1×1 rib as follows:

Row 1 (RS): Sl1 wyib, *p1, k1; rep from * to end.

Row 2 (WS): Sl1 wyib, *k1, p1; rep from * to end.

Rep rows 1 & 2 until piece measures 1" from CO edge, ending with a WS row.

Left Front

Row 1 (RS): Sl1 wyib, (p1, k1) 3 times, p1, knit to last 8 sts, (p1, k1) 4 times.

Row 2 (WS): Sl1 wyib, (k1, p1) 3 times, k1, purl to last 8 sts, (k1, p1) 4 times.

Row 3: Sl1 wyib, (p1, k1) 3 times, p1, knit to last 8 sts, p1, k1, bind off 2 sts, k1, p1, k1.

Row 4: Sl1 wyib, k1, p1, k1, CO 2sts using backwards loop or cable CO, purl to last 8 sts, (k1, p1) 4 times.

Rep rows 1 & 2 until Left Front measures 14 (17, 20, 23.5, 24.5)" from CO edge, ending with a WS row.

Armholes

Next row (RS): Sl1 wyib, (p1, k1) 3 times, p1, k88 (92, 96, 96, 101), BO 38 (42, 46, 48, 48) sts (see Techniques in Glossary for binding off in the center of a row), knit to last 8 sts, (p1, k1) 4 times.

Next row (WS): Sl1 wyib, (k1, p1) 3 times, k1, p19 (23, 23, 25, 26), CO 38 (42, 46, 48, 48) sts using backwards loop or cable CO purl to last 8 sts, (k1, p1) 4 times.

Continue working as established until Center Back measures 13.5 (15, 17, 18, 19)" from armhole BO, ending with a WS row.

Work second Armhole as described above.

Right Front

Continue working as established until Right Front measures 12.75 (15.75, 18.75, 22.25, 23.25)" from armhole BO, ending with a WS row.

Buttonhole

Next Row (RS): Sl1 wyib, (p1, k1) 3 times, p1, knit to last 8 sts, p1, k1, bind off 2 sts, k1, p1, k1.
Next Row (WS): Sl1 wyib, k1, p1, k1, CO 2 sts using backwards loop or cable CO, purl to last 8 sts, (k1, p1) 4 times.

Work 2 more rows as established. Then change to 1×1 rib as follows:
Row 1 (RS): Sl1 wyib, *p1, k1; rep from * to last st, p1.
Row 2 (WS): Sl1 wyib, *k1, p1; rep from * to last st, k1.

Rep rows 1 & 2 until piece measures 13.75 (16.75, 19.75, 23.25, 24.25)" from Armhole BO, ending with a WS row.

Set-up for Tubular BO as follows:
Row 1: *K1, sl1 wyif; rep from * to last st, k1.
Row 2: *Sl1 wyif, k1; rep from * to last st, sl1 wyif.
Rep rows 1 & 2 once more.
Work Tubular BO (see Techniques in Glossary).

Sleeves

Change to DPNs or 12" circulars and work the same for each Armhole.

With RS facing, starting at the underarm and pick up and knit one st in each BO off Armhole st, and then one st in each CO Armhole st. Join for working the rnd, placing m to mark BOR at underarm. 76 (84, 92, 96. 96) sts.

Shape sleeve cap as follows:
Row 1: K42 (48, 52, 52, 54), work GSR.
Row 2: P 7 (11, 11, 7, 11), work GSR.
Row 3: K to 2 sts past prev GSR, knitting ds together, work GSR.
Row 4: P to 2 sts past prev GSR, purling ds together, work GSR.
Rep last 2 rows 13 (14, 17, 17, 18) more times. Knit to end of rnd.

Work St st until sleeve measures 4" from underarm.

Work dec rnd as follows:
Dec rnd: K1, k2tog, knit to last 3 sts, ssk, k1. 2 sts dec'd. 74 (82, 90, 94, 94) sts.

Rep dec rnd every 4th rnd 18 (21, 21, 22, 22) more times. Cont working in St st until sleeve measures 18 (18.5, 18.5, 19, 19)" along underarm (between decreases).

Twisted Rib Edging
Next rnd: *K1tbl, p1; rep from * to end of rnd.
Work twisted rib for 1.5". BO all sts in pattern, or use Tubular BO.

FINISHING
Block pieces to measurements. Add fringe on Left Front, if desired.

FRINGE
Cut 2 pieces of Lunar and 2 pieces of Twig, each 10" long. Hold all 4 strands together and fold in half. Thread through tapestry needle, then thread through left front border, starting at far edge, from front to back. Pull ends through loop to knot. Repeat across the left front, spacing fringe 1" apart.

Sew buttons at shoulders roughly where indicated (on ribbing directly above armhole opening); you may wish to pin buttons in place to determine best placement. Be sure to sew Right Shoulder button on outside of cardigan so fringe is not trapped inside, and left shoulder button on the inside.

Photos pgs 56-57 by Alia Cohn

Local Yarn Stores of Montana

Stix Yarn in Bozeman carries an impressive selection of Montana yarns, as well as a complete line of Brooklyn Tweed and a large stash of Malabrigo. Local yarns include Western Sky Knits, Big Sky, and The Farmers Daughter Fibers. *23 W. Main Street, Bozeman*

Knit 'n Needle in Whitefish is the home of Polka Dot Sheep indie dyed yarns. Shop owner Aimee Alexander founded the shop in 2003 and has been "head dyer" for Polka Dot Sheep since 2011. Polka Dot Sheep is hand dyed locally in Whitefish, and Knit 'n Needle is chock-full of its different bases and colorways. The shop also carries other local Montana yarns, such as Big Sky, as well as Malabrigo, Berroco, Brown Sheep, and others. *14 Lupfer Avenue, Whitefish*

Joseph's Coat Yarns & Fibers is Missoula's oldest local yarn store. It stocks a wide variety of yarns, including Mountain Colors, hand dyed in the Bitterroot Valley, and Montana Sweater Co's Bison Cloud Blend and Bison Ranch Blend yarns. *115 S. 3rd Street West, Missoula*

Yarn Bar carries a wide range of local yarns, many of which are milled at Mountain Meadows in Buffalo, Wyoming. A thoughtful sampling of brands from around the world rounds out the store's selection. A constantly changing rotation of classes and events engages the community and welcomes travelers from far and wide. *1940 Grand Avenue, Billings*

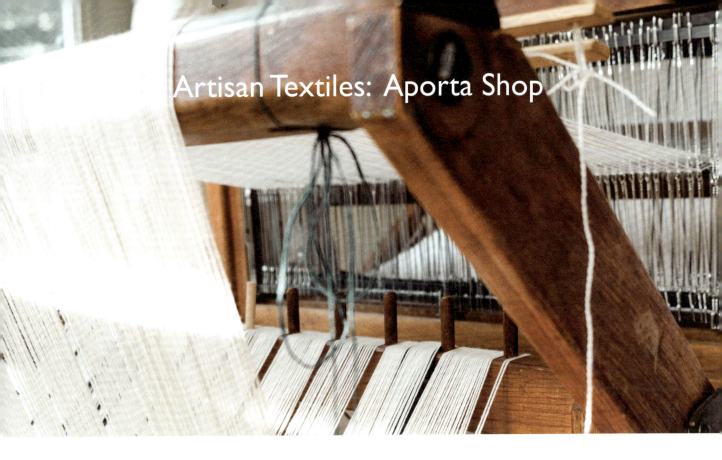

Artisan Textiles: Aporta Shop

It becomes immediately apparent when talking with Noelle Sharp that the depth and breadth of her experience as a fiber artist belies her young age. A knitter since childhood, Noel earned a degree in Fiber Arts from the Art Institute of Chicago, and then founded a company selling handwoven and handknit accessories. Sales led to wholesale accounts and custom design commissions, and then custom designing of textiles for other companies, as well. After time working in Chicago, California, and Manhattan, Noelle found that "I wasn't making art – just manufacturing textiles and running my business. I really missed being in the studio and making art."

Seeking to deepen her knowledge and understanding of fiber and textiles, Noelle sought and was granted a fiber residency in Iceland. Her time there had a profound impact on Noelle's conceptualization of wool and weaving. "Icelandic wool is amazing," she marvels. "It's incredibly warm, and there are so many different ways it can be used. It's not easy to weave with, but I feel like you get almost a watercolor texture when you mix it with a little bit of bulky wool."

Another significant impact on Noelle's development as an artist has been the time she's spent learning to weave from elders in the Navajo Nation. Her work as social media manager for the nonprofit organization Adopt-A-Native-Elder exposed her to Navajo weaving, and her interest was deepened by her work restoring Navajo textiles for the Natural History Museum of Utah. A class at Weaving in Beauty in Gallup, New Mexico led to Noelle obtaining permission to learn a very rare weaving technique taught only amongst certain Navajo families. "The Navajo don't write or draw any of their patterns – they're all memorized," she explains. "The weaving I learned from the Navajo is just for myself – I would never sell that work – but it has intensified my personal weaving practices. Their way of understanding the loom and the textile process has influenced the way I think about designing. It's really intentional, not at all rushed."

textile process has influenced the way I think about designing. It's really intentional, not at all rushed." Noelle describes her current aesthetic a "contemporary minimalist" that combines Icelandic textile influences with some of the Navajo weaving techniques that she has given her own interpretation. She notes the similarity between the values of the Icelandic people and the Navajo: "They both live on the land, and have the utmost respect for their sheep and wool and traditions." And there are similarities between Iceland and Montana, as well - both the reliance on and respect for the land, and how the long, hard winters cause communities to band together and rely on each other.

All of Noelle's skills and experiences have culminated in her next endeavor: opening the Aporta Shop in Missoula. "Missoula has such a strong arts community," she says, "and it needed a space that wasn't art and wasn't craft, but was more design and contemporary craft focus." The Aporta Shop, named after her Danish family's last name, is part artists' gallery, part apothecary, and part a place for the community to learn and to gather together. "I feel like I want to transition into being more of a support center for creatives and textile artists, and then continue my own work, too," she says.

Until the shop opens, Noelle weaves on a 108-year-old loom in her light-filled home studio; current projects include using merino to weave worker bandana scarves, and knitting warm and woolly Icelandic beanies.

Framed pieces woven from Icelandic wool adorn the walls, looking like watercolors painted in fiber, and a table loom holds a partially completed Navajo weaving. Noelle uses her textiles designs to explore color, shape, and form, and the results are hauntingly beautiful.

When Aporta opens, Noelle will move her looms to the shop, so she can work there and teach classes. She has weaving and knitting classes in the works, and plans to invite other textile artists and herbalists to teach, as well. She notes the significant role that the recent resurgence in weaving has played. "Even within the contemporary art world, weaving has a place for itself now. I think people want a closer connection and a deeper understanding of their basic needs – where their food comes from, how their clothing is made. And, from a consumer perspective, awareness of climate change and the slow fashion movement has created a massive transition into being more mindful about the products we're buying. I think people really want that, especially here in Montana, just because of the nature of how we live our lives here. We're intentional, we live off the land, we really depend on our surroundings."

Aporta Shop

Address: 117 W. Front St., Missoula
Website: aportashop.com
Instagram: aportatextiles

Noelle Sharp

Website: noellesharp.com

Botanical Dyeing

Article and Illustrations by Hannah Thiessen

Botanical dyeing is a wonderful way to take advantage of the beauty in a short, but vibrant, Spring and Summer season. In Montana, wildflowers abound during May, June, and July, and the high desert climate makes sure that interesting lichens are ever-present on walks through the fragrant pines. Here are a few of the dye plants used by artisans in Montana and the colors they create.

Yarrow (achillea)
This fragrant plant grows almost everywhere in Montana, and can be characterized by its strong, camphor scent that might remind you of medicine. The yarrow we saw most frequently had bright yellow blooms, reflective of the color you'll get when dyeing with the flower tops. You'll need a 1:1 ratio with this plant but don't over-collect; it's a great pollinator for butterflies and bees. Other names for this plant include Milfoil, Staunchweed, and Soldier's Woundwort.

Purple Lupine (lupinis perennis, lupinis polyphyllus)
You'll want to use the hearty, larger purple lupines for a dyebath, not pink, white, or pale ones. These flowers were ever-present on our hikes on this trip, and are stunning, with large blossom towers that seem to shout to bumble bees and butterflies from even the cool mountain slopes. You'll only want the blossoms for your 1:1 dye ratio, and will notice some of the purple blues rubbing off on your hands as you remove them from the stems (save the stems for a second dye bath that makes beige, tan, and yellow). The varieties you want are known as Mountain Lupine, Wild Lupine, or Large-Leafed Lupine.

Wild Carrot (daucus carota)
Also known as Queen Anne's Lace, be sure not to confuse these common plants with Cow Parsley, Poison Hemlock or Giant Hogweed. Identifying characteristics include a fuzzy stalk and deep purple centers to each umbel (blossom cluster). This dye plant has been used by Indigenous People of the Americas for centuries to get a range of soft yellows, oranges and browns (with an iron modifier), and blends beautifully with other natural colors in weavings. You'll use blossoms and partial stems with a 1:1 dye ratio.

Sheep Sorrel (rumex acetosella)
This plant has little red flowers and a broad leaf, and is loaded with a natural tannin called oxalic acid that doesn't require mordanting. The bath will be a rich reddish color and can yield a variety of tones with a 1:1 or heavier dye stuff to fiber ratio. Expect colors from soft beige and yellow all the way to chartreuse and dark reds and corals. Dip your Sorrel-mordanted fibers into a curly dock bath for potentially stronger reds and corals.

Curly Dock (rumex crispus)
Find these rust-colored, dried stems in fields in late Summer or early Autumn. Chop them up and add them to a dye bath in a 1:1 ratio for a strong color and 1:½ (dyegood) for a weaker color. The weaker bath will yeild beiges and tans, while the stronger bath has a more reddish hue that can be enhanced with an acid modifier like white vinegar or darkened with iron. If paired with a Sheep Sorrel mordant bath before, you can get bright oranges, too.

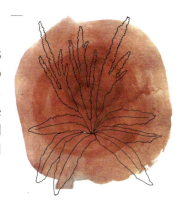

The Process
To naturally dye, you'll need a few basic tools and materials, and it should be noted that while this process uses organic materials, it is not food safe or non-toxic. If possible, work outdoors on a hot plate or use a solar dyeing technique (see below), or if working indoors, work in a well-ventilated space and keep your dye space clear of anything you use for food, cleaning your surfaces off thoroughly afterwards. Your dye pots, spoons, rags, strainers, bowls and anything else you use in your process can only be used for dyeing and should not ever be used again for food--even after washing. We highly recommend picking up beat up used items at thrift and junk shops, as they're the perfect fit for these types of projects!

You'll need:
1-2 large soup pots
Stainless steel or non-stick are okay surfaces, while aluminum and copper can also double as mordanting pots and may affect your final color results in fun and unexpected ways.

A water source
Many dyers save rainwater for dyeing and rinsing, or you can use your water straight from the tap. Keep in mind that in areas where water is more acidic or mineral-heavy, your pH may vary and change your dye results. You can use pH strips, baking soda (or white vinegar) to balance, neutralize, or increase water acidity for different colors.

A mordant
While there are a variety of different mordants and not all dyestuffs require them, most fabrics and fibers will need to be mordanted before they can be dyed. Mordanting prepares your fiber to accept the dyes. Some natural mordants include unsweetened, unflavored Soy Milk, Rhubarb leaves (note, these are very toxic to pets and people and should only be used with an outdoor space), or Aluminum Sulfate (also called Alum, which can be purchased through dye good suppliers like Botanical Colors: www.botanicalcolors.com). The method described below is written with scoured, clean wool and silk in mind. Different steps are required for fibers that still have oils, lanolin, and dirt, or for cellulose fibers like cotton, linen, and hemp.

Mordanting with Alum
Soak your fiber, fabric, or yarn in warm water until fully saturated (usually about an hour). Bring a pot of warm water to a simmer on the stove, and add alum to the hot water at a 15% ratio: for instance, when mordanting 4 oz (100 g) of yarn, you'll need around 1 Tbsp of alum. For wool, you may consider adding 1¼ tsp of Cream of Tartar, as this brightens colors but also helps keep wool fibers softer as they dry (otherwise they can feel a bit crunchy when finished before knit and washed). Dissolve your mordanting ingredients in the water and add your wet dye goods; allow to sit on the heat for 2 hours, but don't allow the wool to boil or bubble. After 2 hours, allow the bath to cool, or extract your textiles and allow them to cool. You can re-use the bath by adding more alum and more fiber as much as you like. When finished, it is safe to dump the bath at the base of plants that enjoy a bit of acidity (like hydrangeas) or down the sink. You can dry and save mordanted fibers for later, or keep them wet to use immediately.

Dyeing
Fill a clean pot with dye goods and enough water to cover your textiles, leaving room for the water to rise as it heats and for textiles to be added later. Most dye goods are used in a 1:1 ratio, so 100g of dye goods is enough to dye 100g of fiber, with a few exceptions for certain potent materials. Bring the water and dye goods to a simmer and allow for 2 hours or more to extract the dye fully. Alternatively, place your dye goods into a gallon-sized mason jar, sealing and sitting it in a sunny window for a week or two; this solar method can yield interesting and different results.

After your dye bath is created, add wet textiles and cook for another 2 hours to allow the fibers time to accept as much dye as possible. Remove from heat and allow the dye goods and water to cool completely, then remove from the dye bath and rinse in lukewarm water until the water runs clear (or as close to clear as you're comfortable with). Hang to dry. For the solar dyeing method, you can strain the dye goods from one jar to another, using the liquid as your dye bath in either a pot or another jar (placing your yarn or fabric inside). If you won't be adding heat, the fibers may need to sit in the dye goods for several weeks to soak up maximum color.

Care
Not all natural dyes have the same longevity when exposed to sunshine or subjected to heavy use. Some fading is normal and part of the beauty of working with these natural materials. Once mordanted, a fiber can be re-dyed several times, so it's always possible to re-dip and wake up the color later in the garment's life! When washing, avoid bleach, and use gentle soaps to preserve color longer.

Lewisia Handwarmers

by Irina Pi

Lewisia is the state flower of the beautiful state of Montana. It is a resilient little plant that can regenerate from a tiny dry piece of root. The flower of the Lewisia is simple in form, which doesn't take away from its beauty. These mittens look simple, but the stitch definition in this soft and luxurious yarn makes them beautiful.

SIZES
Size S (M, L, XL) to fit hand circumference 5–5.5 (6.5–7.5, 7.5–8.5, 8.5–9.5)" / 13–14 (16.5–19, 19–21.5, 21.5–24) cm.

FINISHED MEASUREMENTS
Circumference (unstretched): 4.5 (5, 5.75, 6.5)"
Length: 8.75 (8.75, 11.25, 11.25)"

MATERIALS

The Farmers Daughter Fibers Juicy DK (100% SW Merino; 274 yds per 100 g), 1 skein in Eagle Eye.

US 4 (3.5mm) DPNs or 24" or longer circular needle for working magic loop.

Stitch markers, waste yarn, tapestry needle.

GAUGE

24 sts and 32 rounds = 4" in reverse stockinette stitch, after blocking.

NOTES

Mittens are worked from the bottom up, with increases for the thumb incorporated. The thumb stitches are placed on waste yarn and the rest of the hand warmer is knitted and bound off. The thumb stitches are then picked up to knit the thumb.

Bind off the top ribbing of the hand warmer and thumb ribbing loosely. If your bind off is too tight, switch to a larger needle for bind off only.

STITCH PATTERN

Written Instructions for Central Stitch Pattern Chart (in the round)

Rnd 1: P2, RT, p2, RT, LT, p2, LT, p2.
Rnd 2: P2, Sl1wyib, p3, Sl1wyib, p2, Sl1wyib, p3, Sl1wyib, p2.
Rnd 3: P1, RT, p2, RT, p2, LT, p2, LT, p5.
Rnd 4: P1, Sl1wyib, p3, Sl1wyib, p4, Sl1wyib, p3, Sl1wyib, p1.
Rnd 5: RT, p2, RT, p4, LT, p2, LT.
Rnd 6: Sl1wyib, p3, Sl1wyib, p6, Sl1wyib, p3, Sl1wyib.
Rnd 7: LT, p2, LT, p4, RT, p2, RT.
Rnd 8: P1, Sl1wyib, p3, Sl1wyib, p4, Sl1wyib, p3, Sl1wyib, p1.
Rnd 9: P1, LT, p2, LT, p2, RT, p2, RT, p1.
Rnd 10: P2, Sl1wyib, p3, Sl1wyib, p2, Sl1wyib, p3, Sl1wyib, p2.
Rnd 11: P2, LT, p2, LT, RT, p2, RT, p2.
Rnd 12: P3, k1, p3, k2, p3, k1, p3.

DIRECTIONS

Left Hand

Co 32 (36, 40, 44) sts, pm if needed and join to work in the round.

Cuff

Sizes S & L only:
Rnd 1: *P1, k1; rep from * to end of rnd.

Sizes M & XL only:
Rnd 1: *K1, p1; rep from * to end of rnd.

All sizes:
Rnds 2–14 (14, 18, 18): Rep rnd 1.

Body

Work rnds 1–12 of Central Stitch Pattern as follows:
Rnds 1–12: P2 (3, 4, 5), work chart, p to end.

Thumb Gusset

Rnd 1: PFB, pm, p1 (2, 3, 4), work chart, p to last 2 sts, pm, pfb, p1. 2 sts inc'd.
Rnd 2: P to m, sm, p1 (2, 3, 4), work chart, p to end.
Rnd 3 (Inc rnd): P to 1 st before m, pfb, sm, p1 (2, 3, 4), work chart, p to m, sm, pfb, p to end. 2 sts inc'd.
Rep last 2 rnds 7 (7, 10, 10) more times. Rep rnd 2 once more. Chart rnd 4 (4, 12, 12) last rnd of chart worked.

Separate for Thumb

Rnd 1: P to m, sm, p1 (2, 3, 4), work chart, p to m, rm, transfer the following 18 (18, 24, 24) sts to waste yarn, rm.
Rnd 2: CO 1 st using backwards loop CO, pm for BOR, CO 1 st using backwards loop CO, work chart, p to end.
Rnds 3–19 (19, 26, 26): P1 (2, 3, 4), work chart, p to end.

Ribbing

Sizes S & L only: Rnd 1: *P1, k1; rep from * to end of rnd.

Sizes M & XL only: Rnd 1: *K1, p1; rep from * to end of rnd.

All sizes: Rnds 2–10 (10, 14, 14): Rep rnd 1.

Thumb

With the palm of the hand warmer facing you, return 18 (18, 24, 24) held Thumb sts to needles. Join working yarn and pick up and knit 1 st from the base of the body, pm for BOR, pick up and knit 1 more st from the base of the body. 20 (20, 26, 26) sts.

Rnds 1–6: Purl all stitches.
Rnd 7: *K1, p1; rep from * to end of rnd.
Rnd 8 – 16 (16, 18, 18): Rep rnd 1.

BO all stitches in pattern.
When weaving ends in, close up any gaps around the thumb by weaving the end through the gaps.

Right Hand

Co 32 (36, 40, 44) sts, pm if needed and join to work in the Rnd, placing marker for BOR if desired.

Cuff

Sizes S & L only:
Rnd 1: *P1, k1; rep from * to end of rnd.

Sizes M & XL only:
Rnd 1: *K1, p1; rep from * to end of rnd.

All sizes:
Rnds 2–14 (14, 18, 18): Rep rnd 1.

Body

Work rnds 1–12 of Central Stitch Pattern as follows:
Rnds 1–12: P0 (1, 2, 3), work chart, p to end.

Thumb Gusset

Rnd 1: P0 (1, 2, 3), work chart, p1 (2, 3, 4) pm, pfb, p1, pfb, pm, p to end. 2 sts inc'd.

Rnd 2: P2 (3, 4, 5), Sl1wyib, p3, Sl1wyib, p2, Sl1wyib, p3, Sl1wyib, p to end.

Rnd 3 (inc rnd): P0 (1, 2, 3), work chart, p to m, sm, pfb, p to 1 st before m, pfb, sm, p to end. 2 sts inc'd.

Rep last 2 rnds 7 (7, 10, 10) more times. Rep rnd 2 once more. Chart rnd 4 (4, 12, 12) last rnd of chart worked.

Separate for Thumb

Rnd 1: P0 (1, 2, 3), work chart, p to m, rm, transfer the following 18 (18, 24, 24) sts to waste yarn, CO 2 sts using backwards loop CO, p1, rm, p to end.

Rnd 2: P0 (1, 2, 3), work chart, work chart, p to end.

Rnds 3–19 (19, 26, 26): P1 (2, 3, 4), work chart, p to end.

Ribbing

Work as for Left Hand.

Thumb

Work as for Left Hand.

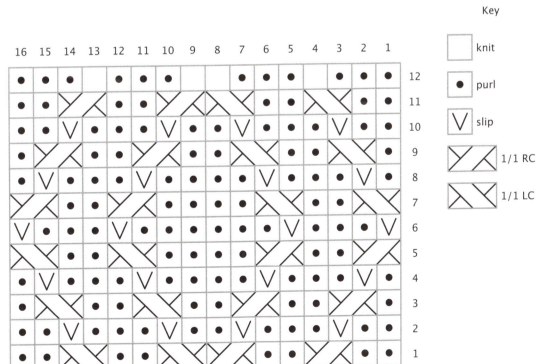

Key
- knit
- purl
- slip
- 1/1 RC
- 1/1 LC

Around Montana

Above and below left: The banks of the Clark Fork.
Below right: Bear grass blooms in abundance throughout Glacier National Park.

From Scratch: Stella German Organic Bakery

There is no way to rush the time-consuming, labor-intensive process of making sourdough bread. In fact, this is one of the many things that Stella Moss loves about bread baking. "I want people to understand that time is such a big part of bread; the value of an endeavor that takes time has gotten lost because we can have anything we want, at any time. But there is value in having to wait." Every Wednesday, Stella starts feeding her sourdough starter. "All I feed it is flour and water," she explains. "The yeast and bacteria are in there and they do their magic. I'm actually still using my original starter, with the original yeast and bacteria colony." By evening, the starter will have grown so much that it will fill a big bucket, and the next morning, Stella begins mixing the dough in a large, commercial mixer.

After the dough is allowed to rise, Stella does "these stretch and folds, instead of kneading, to get the gluten going." Then later that afternoon, she shapes the loaves, tucks them into banneton bowls (which are made of rattan, so that the dough can breathe), and places them in the refrigerator, where they must remain for a minimum of 14 hours. On the third day, she places the loaves into commercial ovens for baking. Some of the loaves go to the Gallatin Valley farmers market, but one-third of Stella's business is now selling directly to customers who come to her home-based bakery to buy loaves of sourdough Polenta, Vollkornbrot (sprouted rye), KAMUT wheat, Purple Corn, and German Rye bread. They're only available on Fridays, and she can only bake about 160 loaves a week, so when they're sold out, there will be no more until the following week.

Stella's love affair with baking began as a child in Germany, baking cookies with her grandmother. Although Stella went on to train as an ornithologist, "I wanted to do something with my hands, where I could see success – an end product. Something I could share with people, because I'm not an outgoing person, but it's a way I could still be involved in a community." Baking allows her to create relationships not only with her customers, but with the farmers who grow bread's most basic ingredient: wheat. To that end,

she is passionate about creating her own supply chain. "If I could, I would grow, clean, and mill all of my own grain!" she laughs. Although that's not yet possible, Stella does source most of her grains – including hard red winter wheat, purple corn, and KAMUT - directly from individual farms, and ensures that they are all organically grown. She also works with Conservation Grains to access a cleaner and a mill.

Stella recognizes that most consumers don't understand the value of freshly milled grain. "Flour on the shelf is dead," she says earnestly, and goes on to explain that when you freshly mill, the flour "has all its nutrients, plus all parts of the kernel. When we buy whole wheat flour at the store, there are pieces missing, to make it shelf-stable. In the beginning, I wanted to tell everyone – I had this need to share this information, to say to people, do you understand what's going on here?" Baking has become Stella's form of activism. "I'm an underground activist in my own way, trying to educate people about bread being such a basic food source." Each loaf embodies the value of taking the time to create a quality product; understanding what your food is made of, where the ingredients come from and how they're grown; and awareness of how fresh, local ingredients both improve food quality and support local farms and ranches.

Stella German Organic Bakery

Baker: Stella Moss

Website: stellabread.com

Instagram: stella_bread

Available at the Bozeman Farmers Market on Saturdays, and direct from the bakery (460 Lower Rainbow Road) on most Fridays

In the Kitchen: Autumn Panzanella

Make use of your last bit of bread with this seasonal chopped salad. Traditionally, panzanella is a Florentine dish that features summertime ingredients like fresh basil, onion, cucumbers and tomatoes, but with the last of a fall harvest just around the corner and sourdough bread to inspire us, it seems a shame to leave this bright dish only for warmer months. Stella Bread's lead baker pulled together a variation featuring fennel and red cabbage that has us dreaming of all of the new ways we could adapt this pastoral dish.

INGREDIENTS AND DIRECTIONS
Croutons
1/4 cup extra virgin olive oil
6 cup bread cubes (about 2/3 of a Polenta loaf works well)
Salt and pepper

Preheat oven to 400F.
Mix the bread cubes with the olive oil in a large bowl. Toss to coat well. Transfer bread cubes to a baking sheet and sprinkle with salt and pepper. Bake, stirring 2 or 3 times, for about 10-15 minutes. Set aside and cool.

Vinaigrette
1/2 red onion, thinly sliced
2 1/2 tbs white balsamic vinegar
Juice of 1/2 lemon

1/4 cup extra virgin olive oil
1/2 tsp Dijon mustard
1 tlb honey

Measure into a little mason jar and shake to combine.

Salad
1 small head of radicchio, torn into bite size pieces
1 small fennel, thinly sliced
2/3 cup parsley
1/2 cup cranberries
1/3 cup toasted pine nuts
3 oz manchego cheese, shaved

Place croutons and all salad ingredients in a bowl and toss with the vinaigrette. Let sit for 30 minutes in the fridge and enjoy!

Glacier National Park

Glacier National Park is one of the country's most stunning national parks, best known for the breathtaking views from Going-to-the-Sun Road and the brilliant blue water of glacier-carved Lake McDonald. Established as a national park in 1910, Glacier is well-known for its diverse wildlife, numerous high mountain lakes, and over 50 glaciers. The Continental Divide splits Going-to-the-Sun Road at Logan Pass, at 6,646 feet in elevation. The historic lodges of Glacier National Park are also a part of the park's heritage, reflecting an early 20th century character. Lake McDonald Lodge, St. Mary Lodge, and Many Glacier Hotel all provide an opportunity to step back in time.

Much of the park is not open to vehicles during the winter months, and Going-to-the-Sun Road typically doesn't open until the end of June. With August forest fires now occurring more frequently, the prime tourist season has been collapsed into a single month: July. As a result, the crowds at Glacier can become unmanageable at times. However, there are parts of the park that are not as popular with visitors, and still provide an ideal backcountry hiking experience. And, as spectacular as Glacier National Park is, it bears remembering that it is surrounded by thousands of square miles of lesser-known parks and national forests that also provide an endless number of hiking trails and campsites, and a chance to experience Montana wilderness with a fraction of the visitors.

"Give a month at least to this precious reserve. The time will not be taken from the sum of your life. Instead of shortening it, it will indefinitely lengthen it and make you truly immortal. Nevermore will time seem short or long, and cares will never again fall heavily on you, but gently and kindly as gifts from heaven." John Muir, 1901.

Swan Lake

Life on the Swan, as locals refer to it, is considered by many to be Montana living at its finest. Slower paced, especially in the winter, there are no large towns or resorts dominating its shores. Often overlooked in favor of Flathead Lake, its larger sister to the west, the Swan stays relatively quiet even during the hectic summer tourist season. Originally founded as a timber camp, recreation is now the big draw here: fishing, boating, hiking, camping, birding, and backcountry skiing in the winter all draw visitors who are looking for more of an off-the-grid, authentic Montana outdoors experience. Huckleberry picking peaks in August, when the state's most-celebrated natural bounty ripens. Spending time on the Swan gives visitors a chance to experience a little of the beauty and solitude that Montana has to offer.

Flathead Lake

The drive down the Flathead Valley from Whitefish to Missoula takes you along the shores of Flathead Lake, the largest natural freshwater lake west of the Mississippi. On both sides of the road, the hills are covered in cherry orchards, and if you are traveling in late July or August, you can stop to pick your fill of Flathead cherries. Hiking, camping, boating, and fishing are all popular activities, and the lake is home to more than 75 species of birds, as well as bighorn sheep and bears. The southern half of the lake is part of the Salish Kootenai Indian reservation. Carved by glaciers during the Ice Age, the lake is fed by the Flathead and Swan Rivers. At around 200 square miles and up to 300 feet deep, it sparkles a deep cerulean blue in the summer sunshine.

Bitterroot Valley

The Bitterroot Valley is nestled between the Sapphire and Bitterroot mountain ranges, and bisected by the Bitterroot River, which runs the length of the valley. A drive from Missoula through the valley opens into large plains, and takes you through charming historic towns like Florence, Hamilton, and Stevensville. The valley was the ancestral home of the Salish tribe of the Flathead Nation, and the Lewis and Clark Expedition followed the Bitterroot River in 1805. St. Mary's Mission, located in what is now the town of Stevensville, was the first white settlement, founded in 1841. Today, the Flathead Indian Reservation is home to the Bitterroot Salish, Kootenai, and Pend d'Oreilles tribes, known collectively as the Confederated Salish and Kootenai Tribes of the Flathead Nation.

One of the Bitterroot's most spectacular features is the thousands of miles of hiking trails and opportunities to view wildlife. In summer, there is world-class fishing, rock climbing, museums and breweries to visit, as well as rodeos, rafting, and mountain biking. There are farmers markets in most every town, culminating in an epic apple harvest each fall. Snowy winters afford opportunities for downhill and cross country skiing, and warm fires in cozy log cabins.

Around Montana

Above: Stormclouds gather over farmland in the Paradise Valley, east of Bozeman.
Below: A peaceful meadow near Echo Lake in the Flathead Valley.

Macramé: Nona & Co

Mackenzie Naegle wasn't yet born when macramé was a ubiquitous presence in every hip, bohemian 1970s home, but she is well aware of the cliché. "I think that artists are reinventing it," she speculates, "so that it becomes our own. I hear the term 'modern macramé' thrown around a lot, and I think the idea is that we can macramé our own interpretation so that it's not forever stuck in the 70s." Mackenzie epitomizes this artistic desire to make what was old new again; inspired by social media images of the knots and twine, she taught herself to macramé from how-to videos. "I was pregnant at the time," she recalls," and feeling very creatively motivated. I needed to make things. I fell in love with how versatile it is – the possibilities for how and what you can make are virtually endless."

When Mackenzie exhibits at art shows and craft fairs, many of the customers who approach her tell stories of trying macramé themselves "back in the day," or watching their mothers macramé. For many, it brings back memories of lazy days at summer camp. "Others just admire it or they want to learn to do it too," she says. "It's really a shared craft."

Mackenzie began learning with clothesline from the local hardware store, recalling that at that time, there weren't as many places to buy materials specific to the art form. Now she primarily uses 5mm single-strand cord, finding that it lends itself well to a variety of uses. She starts sketching the design, to see if the idea in her head will work in actuality. Next, she cuts strands to specified lengths, and then works off of a hanging rack in order to get the tension even. To demonstrate the process, she starts with square knots, "one of the most common macramé knots." She moves on to clove hitch knots, "probably my favorite knot because it allows you to keep things in a uniform line, or it can lend itself to curves."

Much of Mackenzie's work is plant hangers, which are popular at art shows and are very versatile. However, she notes, people love big wall hangings because they're so unique, and one of her biggest selling items is camera straps. She tries to minimize waste by using up all of the scraps for smaller pieces, like earrings. In addition to shows, Mackenize sells her work on Etsy, and hopes to soon incorporate patterns, kits, and summer workshops.

The shop name Nona & Co "pays homage to the makers and crafters who are in my family and have come before me." Both of Mackenize's grandmothers are accomplished makers of knitting, crocheting, and cross stitching, and her maternal grandmother, "mum, as she's called, gave me my first skein of yarn and knitting needles. She and I also share a middle name: Nona. It just seemed fitting to use that." In this way, the shop name also exemplifies the ability of hand crafting to tie together old and new generations of makers.

Nona & Co

Artist: Mackenzie Nona Naegle

Etsy: etsy.com/shop/nonaandco

Instagram: nonaandco

Artwork for sale: Macramé wall art, plant hangers, earrings, camera straps, garlands

Macramé Hanging Planter

Project by Leah Angle of Woven.Vine
Photos by Katie Starks

A bit of greenery brings joy and life almost anywhere, but it's challenging to make room for more house plants with limited floor space or curious pets. Macramé has always been about simple beauty and handmade practicality, and this hanging planter is the perfect pairing with a show-stopping houseplant and handmade vessel (the one we're showing here is from Flourish & Frenzy). Don't fret: these knots are not complex, and this hanging planter is a rewarding first-time macramé project for any skill level.

MATERIALS
(6) 180" pieces of cotton rope
(2) 20" pieces of cotton rope
Metal Ring (needs to be at least 1.5" in diameter, but can be larger)
Scissors
Measuring Tape

KNOTS

Gathering Knot
Gather your cords together::
* With your 20" wrapping cord, make a U-shaped loop at one end and wrap the cord around firmly, over and over again, from top to bottom.
* After wrapping for desired length, place the long end of the wrapping cord (extending from top) until bottom loop disappears under wrapped section.
* Trim the top of excess string off and tuck inside the Gathering Knot.

Square Knot
* Hold an end of the rope in each hand. Pass the right end over and under the rope in your left hand.
* Pass the rope end now in your left hand over and under the one now in your right.|
* Tighten the knot by pulling both running ends at the same time.

Twisted Spiral Knot
* Hold an end of the rope in each hand.
* Pass the right end over and under the rope in your left hand.
* Continue passing the right end over and under the rope in your left hand and you will begin to see the rope make a twisting pattern.
* Tighten the knot by pulling both running ends at the same time.

DIRECTIONS

1. Take the ends of all six pieces of 180" string and pull them through the metal ring. Make sure that the ends of each piece of string are even. You should now have 12 cords extending from the ring.

2. Take one of the 20" pieces of string and create a Gathering Knot around the longer pieces of string.

3. Take 4 pieces of the string and begin your first side of the plant hanger using the pattern listed below.

Pattern for Each Side of the Plant Hanger
Note: The plant hanger will consist of 3 sides. The pattern below is what you will use for each side. My advice would be to complete one side and then move onto the next. That way, you can check to see that each side is measured out consistently with all the sides.

* 3" solid string, no knots
* 5 rows of square knots
* 5" solid string, no knots
* 8 rows of twisted spiral knots
* 5" solid string, no knots
* 5 rows of square knots

4. Measure out 3" below the gathering knot and create a Square Knot. Repeat the square knot 5 times; this will be the start of your pattern.

5. Measure 5" of solid string below your last square knot, then create a Twisted Spiral Knot. Repeat the twisted spiral knot 8 times.

6. Measure 5" of solid string below your last twisted spiral knot, then create a square knot. Repeat the square knot 5 times. *Note: This is the same as Step 4, you are just working further down on the rope.*

7. Repeat steps 3-6 on the other two sides of the plant hanger. Double check as you are working on each side that the distance between each step in the pattern is the same on each side this will help your plant hanger have more of a polished look. *Note: At this point in the process all the sides of the plant hanger should be completed, and you can begin connected the pieces together.*

8. Pull 2 strings from one side and then another 2 strings from another side. Create a square knot using the 4 strings, 3" below the last square knot.

9. Repeat step 8 on the other two sides.

10. Pull 2 strings from one side and then 2 strings from another side. Create a square knot using the 4 strings, 1" below the last square knot. *Note: This will need to be opposite sides from the strings you pulled in step 8. You will want the sides pulled together to resemble a "V", not a large circle.*

11. Repeat step 10 on the other two sides.

12. Pull all the remaining string together and create a Gathering Knot 3" below the last square knot. This is the same as you did in step 1. Make sure the knot is tight and secure so your pot will stay in place.

13. Cut the string to be all the same length below the gathering knot. The string can be as short or as long as you prefer. I like to keep about 2-3". Fringe out the string to create a more bohemian aesthetic or keep as-is.

FINISHING
Place pot and plant inside the plant hanger. Enjoy!!!

#1

#2

Montana Star Quilts

The Native Peoples of the American Plains are well-known for craftsmanship in numerous art forms, including basketry, pottery, woven rugs and blankets, and beadwork. When the wives of Christian missionaries shared their sewing and quilting techniques in the late 1800s, the Plains' Peoples incorporated them into their own textile traditions. This coincided with the near extermination of the buffalo and the tribes' displacement from their native homelands onto reservations. Historically, the giving of painted buffalo hides and robes was a tradition among many tribes as an act of love, peace, and respect. Red buffalo robes were displayed at funerals to honor and protect loved ones on their final journey through the stars. Star quilts replaced buffalo robes in an effort to keep this tradition alive. The act of giving through the dedication and artistry of Native American women's quilting served to honor loved ones and significant moments in a people's history. Quilts were draped on the shoulders of braves and hunters when they returned from battle or a successful hunt, and young men would wrap themselves in a quilt on their vision quests.

Many Indigenous Peoples' legends and oral histories refer to the sky and the stars, and star quilts are sometimes used to tell stories, or the color combinations may have particular meanings. Star quilts are given to show respect and honor, often at sacred ceremonies. The first star quilt was traditionally given at birth, and the last given at death. In modern day, star quilts are still given to graduating college students, men and women returning from military service, newly married couples, or in honor of a special friend or family member. Today, star quilts are featured in school banners, in sweat lodges, and at powwows, and the high school basketball teams on the Fort Belknap Reservation have star quilt giveaways in the style of those on the Fort Peck Reservation.

According to the American Indian Cultural Research Center in South Dakota, "The mythology as well as the traditions of our North American Indian tribes shows a religious observance of the stars and a reverence for all the heavenly bodies. The Milky Way is called the 'Pathway of Departed Souls.' After death it is believed by many that the spirit of the deceased passes on this pathway to the Southern Star, the abiding place of the dead. It is thought that to the Stars, the Great Spirit gave the power to watch over mortals on earth and impart to them spiritual blessings. The Star Quilt is given today as a token of this belief."

Illustration by Hannah Thiessen

Glossary

ABBREVIATIONS

BO	bind off
BOR	beginning of round
CC	contrast color
CO	cast on
dec(s/'d)	decrease(s)/decreased
DPNs	double pointed needles
inc(s/'d)	increase(s)/increased
k	knit
k1 fb	knit stitch through front and then back side of loop, resulting in 1 stitch increased
k2tog	knit 2 together
LT	left twist: insert right hand needle behind the first stitch on left handle needle and knit it through the back loop, then knit the first stitch, slip both stitches off needle
m	marker
p	purl
pfb	purl front and back
pm	place marker
rem	remain(s)
rep	repeat
RM	remove marker
RS	right side
RT –	right twist: insert right hand needle in front of first stitch on left hand needle and knit the second stitch, then knit the first stitch, slip both stitches off needle
ssk	[slip 1 as if to knit] 2 times, insert left needle into fronts of these sts and knit them together
Sl wyib	slip one, stitch purlwise with yarn in back
sm	slip marker
St st	stockinette stitch
st(s)	stitch(es)
WS	wrong side

Opposite page: Even in summer, snow dusts the mountaintops along the Gallatin River.
Back cover: The entire Bitterroot Valley is spread out below, as seen from the Blodgett Overlook Trail.

TECHNIQUES

Binding off in the center of a row tutorial: https://verypink.com/2015/10/21/binding-off-in-the-middle-of-a-row/

Backwards loop CO tutorial: https://blog.tincanknits.com/2013/12/24/backwards-loop-cast-on/

Cable CO tutorial: https://www.purlsoho.com/create/cable-cast-on/

German Short-Rows tutorial: https://www.purlsoho.com/create/german-short-rows/

Tubular BO tutorial: https://www.purlsoho.com/create/long-tail-tubular-bind-off/